WHAT WAS LOST

WHAT WAS LOST

A CHRISTIAN JOURNEY
THROUGH MISCARRIAGE

Elise Erikson Barrett

WJK WESTMINSTER
JOHN KNOX PRESS
LOUISVILLE · KENTUCKY

First edition
Published by Westminster John Knox Press
Louisville, Kentucky

10 11 12 13 14 15 16 17 18 19—10 9 8 7 6 5 4 3 2 1

Scripture quotations, unless otherwise indicated, are from the New Revised Standard Version of the Bible, copyright © 1989 by the Division of Christian Education of the National Council of the Churches of Christ in the U.S.A., and used by permission.

Scripture quotations marked NIV are from *The Holy Bible, New International Version.* Copyright © 1973, 1978, 1984 International Bible Society. Used by permission of Zondervan Bible Publishers.

See "Permissions," p. 161, for additional permission information.

Book design by Sharon Adams
Cover design by designpointinc.com
Cover art: ©iStockphoto.com

Library of Congress Cataloging-in-Publication Data
Barrett, Elise Erikson.
    What was lost : a Christian journey through miscarriage / Elise
Erikson Barrett. — 1st ed.
        p. cm.
    Includes bibliographical references (p.   ).
    ISBN 978-0-664-23520-8 (alk. paper)
    1. Consolation. 2. Miscarriage—Religious aspects—Christianity. 3. Bereavement
—Religious aspects—Christianity. 4. Barrett, Elise Erikson. I. Title.
    BV4907.B37 2010
    248.8'6198392—dc22
                                                              2010003677

PRINTED IN THE UNITED STATES OF AMERICA

♾ The paper used in this publication meets the minimum requirements of the American National Standard for Information Sciences—Permanence of Paper for Printed Library Materials, ANSI Z39.48-1992.

Westminster John Knox Press advocates the responsible use of our natural resources. The text paper of this book is made from 30% post-consumer waste.

For Chris, who has wept with me when it has been time for weeping, and rejoiced with me when it has been time for rejoicing: *devotio perfectio caritatis.*

And to the glory of our beloved and magnificent God, who leads, accompanies, and sustains us on this rich journey.

Contents

Foreword

*B*ooks don't fix everything. They can't. But even if books cannot set every wrong thing straight nor make every painful event reasonable, a good book most certainly can grant us the benison of new thoughts about ancient griefs and long-standing wrong, and this is a good book.

The first principle of a wise book about unfixable things is, then, that its author must accept—and lead us to accept—with humility the fact that in some circumstances the only movement possible is a movement from within ourselves. The chief hallmark of a wise and worthy book about the unfixable is closely akin to that: both the book and its author must respect with quiet and with dignity the sorrow they are addressing. Beyond even both of those traits, however, the thing that most demarcates a good book about loss and pain from an ordinary one is that a good book can form a community—indeed, it almost becomes a community—of those who entered its pages in anger or frustration or grief or resentment or some toxic mélange of those emotions and then came away from those pages less burdened and less defeated.

There is always at least a modicum of the personal in any foreword. Personal presence is understood to be part of the doing of forewords, in fact. But in forewords to books about loss, almost always what is seen and said far exceeds the modest notion of "modicum." Such certainly is the case here.

I am one of those women who, in the days of wine and roses, miscarried over and over again, several times being so far into a pregnancy that we could even know the gender of the child we had just lost. I never have recovered from those losses or ceased to grieve for those children; nor have I ever ceased to identify myself, at least to myself, as one who could not easily bring a pregnancy to term. I suspect that the invitation to write this foreword comes out of the very fact that, not being able to hide my grief, I years ago began instead openly to claim it.

ix

In writing *What Was Lost,* Elise Barrett has done much the same thing, electing not only to claim her grief, but also to record it without self-indulgence and with the kind of grace that, in the hands of the skilled writer, turns personal narrative into communal solace. Because she is an ordained clergywoman, Barrett can and does go beyond the simple sharing of her own, not-too-unusual, physical and emotional experiences with miscarriage. She probes, with informed skill, both the pastoral and the theological implications and ramifications of what presents to the miscarrying woman and her family as random and unnecessary death cast in the stone of an unremitting sorrow. It has been almost unsettling to discover, all these many years later, just how consoled I have been by Barrett's words and insights and lines of thought.

As for that final characteristic of community, already I can hear women like me saying to one another, "Have you read *What Was Lost* yet? It will ease your mind as well as your heart." They are right, it will. And theirs is a company I am grateful to have joined.

Phyllis Tickle

Acknowledgments

I have discovered that it takes both a family and a church to write a book, especially in the gaps between caring for small people. Members of our family, both immediate and extended, took precious vacation days to give me writing time, flew from Indiana to South Carolina to babysit, hosted me and our girls at various homes, contributed funds toward travel and child care, set up work stations in attics and uncles' rooms and their own bedrooms, made meals, gave up naps, and offered all sorts of creative sacrifices to give me the opportunity to write this book. Members of our church, from high schoolers to retirees, came to our home to play with the girls and let me escape to the garage to scratch out another chapter or to edit another section. Being present with tiny people isn't as glamorous as it deserves to be, and so I first want to thank the following persons for the space they helped create for this book to be written: Chris Barrett, Meg and Paul Niehaus, Bob Erikson, Sally and Charlie Barrett, Sandy, Thomas, Caroline, and Ian Moore, Carrie and Renner Langellier, Laura Strong, Mary Em Woods, Sue Runnerstrom, Lindsey Perret, and Miriam Hunter.

I was also graced by the feedback of sensitive, thoughtful readers at every stage of the writing of this book. Thank you to Chris Barrett, Bob Erikson, Jim Erikson, Sandy Moore, Thomas Moore, Charlie Barrett, Sally Barrett, Lisa Schubert, Michael Turner, Karen Westerfield Tucker, and Megan Gray. The time, work, expertise, and insight they offered have made this book so much better than it would have been otherwise.

A group of courageous and generous women agreed to reflect on and share their own experiences of pregnancy loss. Their stories have shaped this book profoundly and have expanded its potential to speak to readers far beyond what I could have created on my own. Most deep thanks go to LeAnn Barnette, Tamara Bennett, JoAnn Chilakos, Heather Dismuke, Katie Free, Christine M. Freeman, Megan Gray, Katherine Hill-Oppel, Lacy W. Johnson,

Susan K. McDonough, Jane S. Mullin, Laura Stern, Debbie Underwood, Molly, Mary, and all other women who submitted interviews.

Sara Brown, whose gripping artwork appears in this book, offered her considerable talent to this project while undergoing treatment for breast cancer and caring for her own daughters. Her grace and courage have blessed me, and I foresee that her willingness to share her own profound reflection in illustrative form will bless others.

Teri Lynn Herbert, research librarian at the Medical University of South Carolina, and Jim Erikson, doctoral student in psychology at Indiana State University, both helped me locate pertinent research and provided me with access to research articles. Dr. Alison Dillon, MD, ob-gyn, MFM, and medical students Ross Strong and Molly Strong read the work with particular attention to medical information and improved my accuracy and understanding immeasurably. Any errors that still exist are mine alone.

Jana Riess, my simply wonderful editor at Westminster John Knox, has shepherded me through the exciting and unfamiliar process of book birthing with grace, good humor, excellent editing and shaping of this manuscript, and timely availability for my questions. It has been a serendipitous gift to have the opportunity to learn from her.

I received word that this book was going to become a reality the day before our younger daughter joined us. The months since then have been both exciting and complicated. My husband, Chris, and my daughters, Emma Ruth and Margaret, have joined forces to help me complete this project. Their flexibility and support have been life-giving and have given me glimpses of what it might look like to fulfill more than one vocation simultaneously. I love all three of you more every day.

Finally, thank you to each person who has encouraged me to write this book in the years since 2003. Pastors recognizing the need for a resource, women and family members frustrated in their search for help—this ministry belongs to you as well.

Introduction

*Y*ou may have picked up this book for any number of reasons. Maybe you had a miscarriage last week, or maybe you had a miscarriage twenty years ago, and you're trying to figure out how to handle the grief. Maybe you saw the word "miscarriage" on the book's spine, and it caught your eye because you have a friend who lost a pregnancy. Maybe you're the spouse or family member of someone who has had a miscarriage, and you're working to find healing words even as you struggle with your own complicated emotions. Maybe you're a pastor doing your best to recognize the loss that one of your church members has experienced. No matter your connection to the topic, I'm glad you found this book, and I pray it proves to be a helpful companion for you.

My name is Elise, and in addition to being a United Methodist pastor, I am a woman who has had multiple early miscarriages. My husband and I experienced our first pregnancy loss while I was still in seminary. I was taken completely aback by how painful it was for me. I had been pregnant for only seven weeks, but still it seemed as though my heart, my sanity, and my life were all splitting into pieces. And so, in my role as full-time student, I tried to deal with my grief and confusion by studying all that had been written about miscarriage. It didn't take long. Don't get me wrong; there are a few good resources available, some medical, some psychological, some spiritual, and I will point you toward some of the books and articles I found helpful. But I could find very little of what I really needed—reflections about questions like, "Where was God?" "Did this little life matter to anyone but me?" and "Why does everyone keep telling me that there was a reason for this?"

When we lost that first pregnancy, I had rarely heard anyone else talking about miscarriage, yet approximately one in four pregnancies will end in miscarriage. Why didn't these two things match up? I didn't know of many other people who had been through something similar, but that changed quickly. My experience was a little like a password into a secret society. As people discovered that I'd had a miscarriage, all sorts of women and men would quietly sidle up to me and say, "We lost our first baby too," or "I had three miscarriages fifty years ago." This kind of loss has touched so many people, and yet we don't seem to have ways of talking about it.

Even in the church—perhaps especially in the church—we Christians have a tough time knowing what to do with miscarriage. We know how to have baby showers, how to bring casseroles and rock new babies and crochet booties. An infant death or stillbirth, while unspeakably tragic, carries rituals: a funeral, a visitation, bereavement cards, and flowers. But we don't know what to do for people who have lost pregnancies before a baby ever appeared.

This book is meant to be a companion on the journey through a complicated grief for those whose pregnancies have ended too soon. You will notice that I share a great deal of my own story within its pages. This is not intended to serve as an example of what pregnancy losses *should* feel like. Far from it. Instead, my hope is that as you read about my own experiences and those of other women, you will be better able to sort through and tell the story of your own experience. Think of it as a conversation we're beginning. Every person's experience of this loss will be fundamentally different. There are no shoulds, no oughts, related to your feelings.

The book is set up so that, if you choose, you can use it as a reflection guide. Each chapter ends with questions for reflection as well as an exercise you can try. One way to use the book would be to read one chapter at a time, and then spend quiet time for the next few days reflecting on that chapter. You could write in a journal in response to the reflection questions and spend time doing the exercise outlined. You also could use this book in the context of a support group or other small group.

Don't feel compelled to do any of these things, however, if they are not comfortable for you. This book is meant to be a companion for you in your grief, not a boss. If you don't like journaling, you could find a trusted person to talk through those questions with you—a friend, pastor, counselor, or spouse, or even a pregnancy loss support group. The goal is to find a way to tell your own story, as I will share mine with you in these pages. Sharing our stories helps us process what has happened, understand what we're feeling, and move through the pain we're experiencing. And sharing our stories helps those around us understand how best to support and love us and how to be with others who have lost pregnancies.

I hope that this book can support and help you as you share your story of loss. I also hope that it will help you turn to God for support and help. This is a Christian book, and my deep hope is that using it will provide a path for you to remain in relationship with God during this painful time. You may be angry at God, or disappointed in God, or wondering if God even exists at all. These are all normal emotions (even for God's children—just look at the Psalms!) and God can handle them. We will talk about this more later, but for now it's enough to say that your pain matters to the One who made you, and that God wants to make this journey with you—no matter what state you're in.

Because the chapters follow chronologically, your reading will make most sense if you read the chapters in order. However, because they are organized topically as well, you are welcome to read the ones that seem most necessary to you at different times. Share this book with your loved ones and friends, if you think there are parts that will be helpful to them as they do their best to love and support you. The last chapter contains resources for ongoing reflection, including other recommended reading and complete worship and memorial service resources.

One final story before we begin. I was serving as a pastor at a downtown church when a woman who had lost a pregnancy at twelve weeks came into my office. Her first stop had been a local Christian bookstore. She kneaded damp Kleenex on her lap as she said to me, "There wasn't anything! Not a thing! They had books on healing from abortion, books on pregnancy, books about children, but nothing about miscarriage! Am I the only person to ever have trouble dealing with this?" She is not the only one—far from it. This book is for her, and for people like her, and for people who love people like her. I pray that it will help you walk through this grief, and I pray that it will help you trust God again.

Feast Day of St. Catherine of Siena
2009

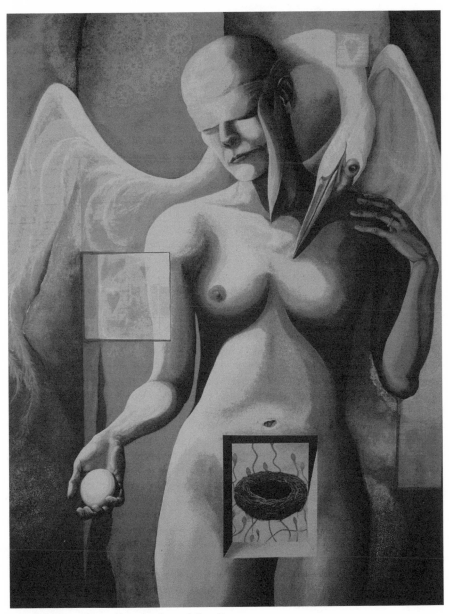

"The Gift," 40 x 30 acrylic and collage, © Sara Brown.

PART 1 The Journey through Miscarriage

Chapter 1

Remembering Your Pregnancy

I was twenty-four years old when my husband and I were married, an idealistic twenty-four, commuting three hours one way to Durham, North Carolina, to finish my divinity degree. During the week, I lived in northern Durham, in the basement of a 1960s split-level home with a couple in their seventies, and on the weekends I returned to our brick ranch parsonage, a newlywed in the town of Blacksburg, South Carolina, population two thousand. In most ways this schizophrenic life was pleasant, and it proved to be a very good way to work into matrimony. Chris and I were always delighted to see one another, and we would throw ourselves into the work of being married on the weekends with verve and good humor—"Why don't I clean the bathroom this time, sugar?" We talked over the foibles of parishioners and professors, chummily red-inked his sermons and my papers, ate homegrown tomatoes dropped at the back door by church members, played with our doe-eyed pound dog, and were as happy as two people could reasonably be.

I think that this was why natural family planning was perhaps less effective for us than for others. I had explained the method to my mother with great enthusiasm, and then defended it vigorously when she hopefully suggested that I might want to try the Pill. I had tried the Pill, I said, and it made me feel like Medusa—bad temper, snakes, and all. I was going to chart, and we were not going to get pregnant, not while I was in school.

But all it took was one inattentive weekend reunion, and I was staring at two lines on a dollar-store pregnancy test.

I was a bit shocked. But secretly, I was thrilled: more thrilled, in fact, than I thought I really ought to be. Practically, this made no sense. I was living in two places, going to school full-time, and almost all of Chris's small salary was making its way to Durham with barely a stopover in our checking account. All the same, I was thrilled. We're married, after all, I'd tell myself, as smiles I couldn't control stretched across my face. I have a secret,

I thought. I am full of a secret. I am blossoming, fertile and lovely, and I am holding life inside of me.

That next week, when I returned to school, I was bubbling over with that life. It was such a transformative thing—I was going to have a baby!—and I couldn't imagine not preparing the way for that transformation. Like a bulldozer before a road crew, I crashed seriously along the paths I walked at school. I had a meeting with the academic dean, inquiring about the pros and cons of switching from the three-year program I was in to a two-year master's degree program. I spoke gravely to my four professors, warning them about the probability that I would need time off, that sometimes I might not be able to make the drive. When I stayed after class to explain the situation to one of those professors, he broke into smiles and told me about his joy in becoming father to two small children. "It will change your life," he said. I smiled too. It already had. I was a part of this happy club of people who were parents, Christian parents, taking the blessing of procreation and the obligations of discipleship seriously.

And I did take those things seriously. I felt as if I finally understood the exhortation in 1 Thessalonians to "pray constantly." Every moment was a prayer, every moment charged and filled with awareness of the tiny life growing inside me. Every time the bread and juice of Communion touched my lips, I felt a searing connection to this mysterious little being inside me, who was receiving Communion along with me. Every step I took on the fifteen-minute walk to and from the remote parking lots assigned to divinity school students—every crack in the sidewalk avoided, every soft landing from a curb, every careful check of oncoming traffic—every second was a prayer breathed and answered. My hands, almost on their own, would float to my slightly bloated belly, barely touching it in benediction twenty times a day. I would wake up in the morning in the basement I occupied and smile, and pray, "O God, I know I should be scared, and this timing is really not what we'd planned . . . but God, I am so thankful. I am thankful because you made marriage for blessings like this and we are indeed full of blessing."

Because I felt so heavy with blessing, I took my care of that blessing very seriously as well. I packed my backpack with healthy snacks—bananas, which I hated, but which seemed extra virtuous for that very reason; cashews, which were a terrible expense but so nutritious—and I carefully avoided alcohol and caffeine, which seemed to show up in all sorts of innocent-looking places, like chocolate. I pored over the recommended diets and even photocopied one for the refrigerator, so I would be sure to have representative calories from all the important categories. As I filled my stomach with bananas and spinach and milk and whole wheat, I became more aware of responsibility and joy. These bananas were for the baby. That spinach was for the baby. I would go to sleep early for the baby. I luxuriated in the new obligations. I thanked God for the chance to prove that I would be a good mother.

Since I was attending Duke and had student health coverage, we decided that I would find an ob-gyn there, even though I likely would deliver the baby in South Carolina. So I made an appointment to have the pregnancy confirmed at the student health clinic. My roommate from my first year accompanied me, and we explored the maze that is Duke Hospital, looking for the proper administrative window. Sitting there, waiting for my name to be called, Christy looked at me and said, "Aren't you scared?" Yes, I said, I was, but also thrilled. I had this completely irrational fear, however, that the official pregnancy test would be negative, and that all of my impressive preparations would look simply silly, the overreaction of a fertile imagination. I provided the requested urine sample, a little clumsily, and tried to seem nonchalant as Christy and I leafed through magazines. The nurse finally called me back and sat me down, and said, "Elise, the test is positive." Her plump face was creased and creased again with her smiles. She continued, "This is wonderful; it's so seldom I get to tell students this as *good* news!" Good news, I thought, glancing at my wedding band. Wonderful news. And now it was *official* good news! If Duke Hospital said I was pregnant, there could be no doubt. They scheduled me for my first appointment six weeks later.

Turning pages in my calendar later that night, back in the snug basement of the home I shared with the grandparent-like couple, I not only wrote down that appointment, I also wrote down every milestone I could think of on the way to a baby. "Two months pregnant!!" I wrote, with a little smiley face. "Six months pregnant!" "Baby due!!" with a heart around it. Of course, I wrote in pencil, knowing that dates could change. But I imagined what would be happening at each of those milestones: what I'd miss at school about the time of our ultrasound, what the weather would be like when the baby arrived. A September birthday would be lovely, I thought. Parties would be so much fun—we could have people play outside, and it would still be nice and warm.

When I got home that weekend, Chris and I called our parents to tell them the pregnancy had been confirmed. Joy and rapture on both sides. My mother offered to give us my little brother's old crib, and Chris and I wandered through the parsonage, discussing the pros and cons of each bedroom as a nursery. We finally decided on the middle bedroom in the hallway, the one with twin beds in it. It had two windows on one wall and was just the right distance from our room. I thought we could paint it blue, and I mentally sketched out where we would put the crib and a changing table.

When we sat by the fire later, in our wood-paneled den, we talked about how amazing it would be to have a baby there, playing on the Berber carpet, snuggled up at night, crying to wake us to eat. We were wide-eyed and overwhelmed, trying to imagine all the things we had heard people talking about, trying to imagine the feel of a sleeping newborn, the smells of milk and diapers, the sounds of crying and gurgling and laughing. I fell asleep that night smiling, my hand resting on the bit of skin and flesh that covered the little life inside me.

Looking back, this all seems very naive, but there is something both magical and terrifying about a first pregnancy. We know, if we know anything about children, that living with small people is going to mean a permanent and profound change, so it's only natural for expectant parents to start preparing themselves for that change by planning and using their imaginations. Then there are the physical changes for the mother. Your body is changing in unexpected and uncontrollable ways: your digestion changes, your breasts swell and start to hurt, funny veins start popping out all over the place, your stomach gets queasy, you have headaches or strange sensations. You start to have unpredictable emotional responses to normal comments your husband makes, crying every time you see a certain cell phone commercial. And if you don't know much about miscarriage, if you or someone you are close to has not experienced a pregnancy loss, you have no sense of anything but inevitability about the outcome. We are scared away from sex from adolescence on by the *threat* of a baby, we remember occasional alarmist articles in teen magazines about girls who got pregnant "just from oral sex!"—no wonder it rarely occurs to us that it may, in fact, be possible to be pregnant without having a baby at the end of nine months. This is why, for many women, miscarriage comes as a terrible, unwelcome surprise, something they never knew they should fear. Tammy, who lost her second pregnancy to miscarriage, put it this way:

> I had prayed for so long and was so excited that God had answered my prayer by giving me a second child. I was very maternal from the beginning and jumped the gun on getting things ready for the new baby to come. I had one child and had followed all the rules about not getting things together (maternity clothes, baby items, etc.) too soon with my first pregnancy and just thought I'd enjoy the experience a little earlier this time around. [I] had no idea or thought that I might lose this child. My first pregnancy was "perfect."

In twenty-first-century America, we also tend to assume that we have an enormous amount of control over the process of becoming pregnant and having children. We have medications, pills, condoms, and fertility drugs that many of us vaguely imagine have the power to regulate the process perfectly. This assumption is only confirmed if you are able to become pregnant easily. JoAnn shared about her first pregnancy:

> When I got married at the tender age of twenty, back in June 1963, I was naive enough to believe that all of our hopes and dreams would come to pass on our time schedule, and at our request. . . . I guess my first experience with this unrealistic thinking came on July 25, 1967. My husband (at the time) and I had decided that upon my graduation from college in 1965, we would wait about two years, save the money I'd earn from teaching, and then start a family. When it was determined that I was pregnant, in April 1967, we were ecstatic. How wonderful . . . how easy . . . how convenient! Even the due date given, of December 15, 1967, was perfect. I'd be able to take an extended Christmas/maternity leave, and we'd have a "Christmas baby."

If pregnancy does happen easily, we can be lulled into even more of a false sense of control over the whole journey of procreation, making miscarriage an even greater shock. One woman said:

> After being married four years, my husband and I decided to have a baby. I felt so blessed to become pregnant after only trying for one month. When I was able to attempt another pregnancy, I became pregnant after two months. Both times, I felt God had blessed me with good health to be able to become pregnant so quickly. Babies are one of the greatest miracles from God.

Katherine offered, "I do feel that God touched me in order to create our babies' lives/souls." When God's hand is sensed at work in conception, miscarriage can come not only as a shock, but also as a crisis of faith, when our sense of God's control and our control over the process is shaken.

We have longer than ever before to get ready, as well. Even within the past five years, and definitely within the last fifteen, home pregnancy tests have become more sensitive and readily available, fundamentally changing how we find out we're pregnant. Twenty years ago, the missed period was the first sign, but a woman who miscarried early would probably chalk it up to a menstrual cycle that started late. Women were having miscarriages regularly, but many fewer women knew about it. The process of planning and imagining started later, after a trip to the doctor, after the likelihood of miscarriage was already reduced.

Now, stacks of boxes in the family-planning section of drugstores and groceries boast boldly lettered promises: "Test as early as 5 DAYS before your missed period!" We have the gift of finding out so very early when a fertilized egg has implanted and begun growing, and so we have also the burden of knowing about many pregnancy losses we would not have known about otherwise. Furthermore, many women are waiting longer than ever to start having children, waiting until lengthy education programs are completed, until a career is established or a move is made. The average age of women having their first child went from 21.4 years in 1970 to 24.9 in 2000.[1] We are having first children later in life, and older mothers have a statistically higher rate of miscarriage.

Every single one of us approaches that pregnancy-test aisle in the drugstore with different feelings. Some women, like me, are thrilled by the possibility. It comes as a happy surprise or an answer to prayer, and the test seems to open the door to all sorts of wonderful future dreams and visions. Others are scared to death to crack open the stick and see what it says. Maybe you were one of these women. Maybe for you, pregnancy came as something fearful, whether expected or not. Perhaps you weren't married, or didn't have a partner you could rely on to be committed to you and the child. Or perhaps you were married or engaged but feeling trapped in an unhealthy or unhappy relationship, and having a child felt like it would have cemented the misery. Maybe your relationship was fine, but your partner didn't want to have a child. Maybe you felt as though you weren't ready to be pregnant, that this was going to be the end of everything you'd hoped for and worked toward in your career. Maybe the pregnancy itself was miserable: you didn't want the baby, and you felt trapped by the changes happening in your body. Or maybe you experienced some combination of feelings: both excited and worried, both happy and miserable, both looking forward to and regretting the impending change.

Other women have been trying hard to get pregnant for months, or even years. If you are one of these women, you probably brought home your test (value-pack-sized, those "buy three for the price of two" packages) full of hope, but already anticipating disappointment. And when the test told you that you were finally (finally!) pregnant, you may have been full of other emotions. Maybe you tried not to get your hopes up too quickly, especially if you had had disappointments before. Maybe you didn't believe the first test and took another one to be sure. Maybe you made an immediate appointment with your doctor, to do everything you could to cement this fragile miracle. Maybe you were worried sick about the two and a half drinks you'd had at a wedding reception before you knew, when you were still telling yourself, "It hasn't happened yet—why should this time be any different?" Maybe you were simply ecstatic to finally be pregnant and eager to spread the news. Heather shared, "With my first pregnancy (and loss), I had been dealing with infertility for nine years and became pregnant . . . with [this pregnancy] we told everyone since we were so excited after all those years of infertility."

Every woman's story is different. Every woman's pregnancy is different. But for every one of us, it makes a difference in our lives, and thinking about that difference helps us recognize what was lost when the difference died.

REFLECTION QUESTIONS

1. Reflect on your own pregnancy. How did you find out you were pregnant? How did you feel? How did your partner respond to the news?
2. How was your relationship with God affected by the pregnancy? For example, did your prayers change? If you attended church while you were pregnant, did your experience of worship change? Did you feel closer to or farther away from God during your pregnancy?

EXERCISE

Think of someone who would be a good conversation partner for you during this time—your spouse, a close friend, a trusted pastor or church member, another woman who has lost a pregnancy, or a counselor. Ask that person if you can tell her or him the story of your pregnancy. Share with your conversation partner what the pregnancy meant to you, how you felt about expecting a baby, and what you did to start preparing, in emotional, mental, and physical ways.

Chapter 2

Remembering Your Miscarriage

*S*undays are a little intense in most pastors' homes. And Chris was serving what's known as a two-point charge, in which one pastor serves two churches. The two churches we were part of for those years were in many ways quite different. One was downtown, a graceful turn-of-the-century brick building in the shadow of First Baptist Church, with stained-glass windows and creaky-floored Sunday school classrooms. The other was out in the country, a twelve-mile drive up to a local "mountain," and looked for all the world like the church immortalized in that old tune "The Little Church in the Wildwood." It still boasted a bell in the churchyard, a relic from the days when the circuit preacher would ride into the community on horseback and the bell would be rung to call folks in from the fields to listen to the preaching. Each church had its own flavor, each was full of personality, and each sheltered the prayers and common life of between thirty and forty saints and sinners.

The idea behind having a two-point charge is that the membership of those churches is small enough to allow the pastor to care for each approximately half-time. The challenge, of course, is that usually a two-point (or three-point) charge does not have the funds to hire, say, a secretary or administrative assistant. So the pastor is responsible for doing everything from visiting and preaching to preparing bulletins and filling out administrative forms. This meant that Sundays with my darling procrastinator of a husband were always exciting. He would rise before sunlight started sneaking over the foothills and work intently in front of the computer, books and commentaries and notes strewn wildly around his feet, one leg jiggling frantically as he looked for just the right word, tried to find the perfect example or metaphor, something that would bring the Scriptures to vivid freshness in that morning's sermon. At some point, we would have breakfast (I in the sunny nook in the kitchen, he in the bedroom/office) and he would update the bulletins.

We would look up last week's statistics—thirty-eight in attendance for worship, $748 collected—and put those into their proper spots. He would settle on a sermon title, write a pastoral prayer, and hit "print," and we'd whirl out the door, his black robe flapping around long legs.

I usually drove to the churches, and our routine was invariable. The only driver breaking the speed limit at 7:50 on a Sunday morning, I'd sling the car onto the side of the street outside the downtown church and leave it running as Chris ran inside to leave the freshly printed order of worship on the photocopier for some devoted layperson to run during Sunday school. He would dash back out, I'd accelerate madly down the gravelly back roads, and as he folded still-warm sheets of paper in tilted halves and reviewed his sermon, we'd screech into the tree-sheltered parking area at the country church, usually with bare minutes (or seconds) to spare before worship began.

The first few minutes in worship after all this excitement were always peaceful. Some Sundays I'd sing in the choir, using the old 1920s Cokesbury hymnal; most Sundays I would stay in a pew, on the left side about a third of the way back. I would decorously receive a bulletin from the gracious hands into which Chris had thrust the stack of them moments before and fit my body into the wooden L of the pew. My eyes would scan the order of worship as if for the first time, and I would grow quiet, readied by the sounds of feet on old wood, creaking doors, and folks speaking quietly in soft rural South Carolina drawls.

The Sunday I lost the pregnancy started the same as all the other Sundays. The only difference was that I'd had some faint spotting earlier that morning, when I was getting ready. I had done a frantic Internet search and found plenty of sites that assured me that all was (probably) well. And so I had gotten ready just as usual, with just a nagging uncertainty in the back of my mind that distracted me as I responded to the call to worship and sang the hymns. As soon as I politely could after the service, I ducked across the churchyard to the small fellowship building where the bathrooms were located and checked again. A little more spotting, but still nothing to be worried about, I told myself.

Because I really thought everything was all right, then, I was unprepared when cramps started to twist my abdomen during the service at the second church. I knew then that something was terribly, terribly wrong, but I didn't know exactly what. I vividly remember staring at the black words and musical notation on the thin pages of the hymnal, unable to concentrate enough to understand what they meant. After what seemed like an eternity, worship was over and Chris and I pushed open the door of the parsonage. I went to the bathroom and saw blood. I changed clothes and went to my tired husband and said, "I think I'm having a miscarriage."

He looked up at me, sitting on the side of the bed, one shoe off and one shoe on, in his shirtsleeves, and he was silent for a moment. Then he put his shoe back on, got up, put his hand on my shoulder, and said, "Well, let's go to the hospital." He paused. "Is that what we do?"

I nodded, and we got into the car. Chris drove faster than he should have, with the result that the forty-five-minute drive to the hospital took closer to thirty-five minutes. The ride was mostly silent. I was numb, repeating in my head, "Please, God . . . please, God," and there didn't seem to be much point to talking. We parked close to the emergency room and walked along the sidewalk to the door. The glass panel slid to one side, and we stepped inside the unbelievably crowded waiting room. *Of course*, I remember thinking, *it's Sunday afternoon.*

We gave our names to the harried intake staffer, found seats (though none were available side by side), and began waiting.

From this point onward, I can't remember what happened very well. My memories come in short clips. Trips into the filthy bathroom, looking, dazed, at dark red blood on the pad I'd grabbed before we left the house. Flipping the pages of the few free circulars that were strewn around the waiting room. Being called back for a triage interview, feeling frantic that it was taking so long, but with a hopeless knowledge at the pit of my stomach that it wouldn't matter how long it took, that there was nothing they could do. My sweet husband checking, checking, checking with the front desk to make sure we hadn't been forgotten. It was well over two hours before we were finally called back to get an ultrasound.

I had to have a reverse catheterization, an unpleasant enough process, but the results were even worse. The technician, in a mournful riff on the "first ultrasound" mystique, forced fluid into my bladder, squeezed cold gel on my stomach, and rubbed the wand around silently for several moments. "Hmm," she said. "Well, there's nothing there, not that I can see . . . but it's possible that you're just much earlier along than you thought you were." I knew better. One of the benefits of charting for birth control was that I knew precisely when everything happened. I knew when I had gotten pregnant, and I knew how far along I should have been. And I knew then that the baby was gone.

In a daze, we were shepherded to another examination room to wait for a doctor. While we were waiting, two things happened. The first was that, much like grieving people at a wake, we started making gruesome and sad jokes. The second was that a pastor friend came to see us. Mike was a generation older than we and had supervised Chris for a summer internship while Chris was in school. While we were in the waiting room, I had not felt up to calling our parents, either set of them. But Chris had asked if he could call Mike, who was serving a church a few blocks from the hospital. Embarrassment struggled with the need to turn the spiritual side of this over to someone else, and that need won. I told him he could call, and just as we were settled in the examination room, Mike arrived.

God bless him, he was wonderful. Mike, a short, stocky, white-haired fellow with a perpetual smile creasing his face, walked in, his smile full of concern and sympathy. He hugged Chris, came over to squeeze my hand, and listened silently as we told our brief story. I can't remember if he said anything wise, but I do remember how solid and comforting his presence was, how incredible the relief was when he walked in. Looking back, I think it was because Chris and I, usually professional pray-ers, professional "presence of God" types, were too bruised and bewildered to be able to deal with God in that moment. Just knowing that there was someone there who could believe in God for us for a little while, who could pray for us and be confident for us, felt like someone had put a warm, heavy blanket around my shivering shoulders.

The three of us visited for a while, talking about nothing in particular, until the doctor entered the room, a kind young woman with dark hair and a tired face. She examined me and looked at the ultrasound results, and sighed. "We just can't be absolutely sure at this point, you understand," she explained to me. "It's probable that you've lost the pregnancy, but in case there's still a chance, I want to take precautions." Precautions, it became clear, primarily involved no pain medications and no tampons. I was to go to the hospital's ob-gyn practice early the next morning and wait to be worked in. They would do blood work, and the comparison would tell us for sure.

Mike and his wife, Donna, asked if we wanted to stay with them that night, and Chris and I were so dazed that we didn't even hesitate politely. Just as Mike's presence in the hospital room had felt like a warm blanket, the door to their parsonage seemed like the entrance to a fallout shelter. For some reason, my most vivid memories of that night center around walking into their home—Donna's brisk and cheerful hospitality rolling out in front of our feet, a beautiful, time-polished oak sideboard in the kitchen that had belonged to her grandmother, Chris and I sitting on their couch. I tried to erase thought by flipping through a copy of *Southern Living* that was on the coffee table. "Apple pie like grandma used to make," I read, as cramps assailed me again. "Time to plant hydrangeas."

The rest of that night passed the way any nightmare does. I sat upright in the bed, shoved into a sitting position by a pile of pillows, almost dozing between cramps (contractions?), and then being awakened unmercifully as the intensity increased. I took trip after trip to the bathroom, changing soaked pads, watching helplessly as clots began to pass with the blood. And I cried, half asleep, slow tears washing my face as I wondered if our baby had been a boy or a girl.

The next morning found me wandering tentatively around Spartanburg Regional Medical Center, looking for the obstetrician's office while Chris parked the car. It was a large practice, thirteen doctors, and I finally found the glass door at the end of a nondescript hallway. I pushed my crumpled emergency-room paperwork that shouted, "spontaneous abortion!" across the desk, and a receptionist with a carefully blank expression invited me to have a seat in the waiting room, saying that they would work me in when they could.

I tried to find the most inconspicuous seat in the waiting room, averting my eyes from the huge, baby-filled bellies I seemed to see everywhere I looked. I felt simultaneously like a harbinger of doom—"Look out, not all pregnant people end up with babies!"—and horribly, sickly jealous. Hiding close to the stacks of magazines, I began leafing through glossy publications with names like *Your Baby Today*, *Babyhood*, *Parenting*, *Mother and Child*. After a few minutes, I realized that I was going to start crying in a fairly open and attention-getting way if I kept looking at these articles, and so I looked to see if there was something else. Nary a copy of *Golf* was to be seen. "What do the women here for hysterectomies read?" I asked Chris as he joined me, and found a dog-eared copy of the hospital's publicity publication, which I read over and over until my name was called, more than an hour later.

The doctor, a large, gentle, middle-aged man, was as kind as he could have been. I told him as I came in, "I know you have to test, but I already know I've had a miscarriage," as if claiming the sad news up front would make it better when the lab proved it, kind of like breaking up with your high school boyfriend before he has a chance to break it off with you. After the examination and blood work had been completed, the doctor invited me to sit down in his office, and said, "You were right, and I'm sorry. You have lost the pregnancy." Tears, hot and embarrassing, welled to my eyes, and I said, "I know—it's fine—I'd be fine if the cramping didn't hurt so much. Can I have some sort of painkiller now?" The doctor, understanding, gave me a mini Snickers bar and a box of Kleenex, and went out to get me some ibuprofen. When he came back, the pills in a little white paper cup, he said, "It's quite normal to grieve this, you know." I interrupted with something like, "Well, I was only seven weeks along," and the doctor continued, "The truth is, there have been studies done, and the grieving process is actually quite similar no matter how advanced the pregnancy is." This was absurdly comforting. In the halls of science and empirically verified truths, I received the news that science had given me permission to feel this wrenching hurt and emptiness and bewilderment with some sort of strange satisfaction. I left the office and trudged to the car, numb, adjusting to a new life I wasn't sure I liked very well. The months rolling out before me had seemed very full; now they were suddenly empty. I had been a mother-to-be; now I was not even sure I would ever be a mother. Our baby was gone before she had ever arrived, and I felt as if I'd been wrenched out of someone else's life, a life brimming with promise and abundance and joy, and deposited back in a barren place I thought I'd left behind.

What was your own miscarriage like? I've heard stories of many different experiences of pregnancy loss. In most of them, women talk about that period of time between fearing and being sure that the pregnancy could not be saved; they talk about the pain, and they talk about the blood. Maybe you will relate to LeAnn's experiences:

> With the loss of our first baby at about eleven weeks, I experienced overwhelming sadness. I had begun to have some bleeding and went in for an ultrasound. It was a Friday afternoon, and once the doctor told us we were losing our baby, he sent me home to miscarry on my own (to avoid having a surgical procedure). This was a physically painful and emotionally draining weekend . . . by Sunday evening I had lost the baby.
>
> My second miscarriage experience was quite different from the first. . . . Again, I began experiencing some bleeding around the tenth week. It was a Friday, and my doctor's office closed around eleven. I called the office around ten, but they wanted me to lie down for a while to see if the bleeding would stop. Of course it didn't, and I went to the ER later that evening with the understanding that I would see the doctor on call from my ob-gyn office. That didn't work out, and a stranger delivered the news that our baby was no longer living. This time, my experience was filled with anger. Again, I was sent home to miscarry on my own. This time, it took nearly three weeks!

Some women even experience premonitions, feelings that something is wrong before they have any physical evidence. Mary told a haunting story:

> [My miscarriage] started at school. It was the week before finals and I was finishing up not only the year but also the end of the job. I knew something was wrong. I was ten weeks out. I was supposed to get my first ultrasound the following week. I knew it wasn't just spotting.
>
> The night before I had a terrible nightmare that I haven't told anyone until just now because it was so horrible and so prophetic I didn't think

anyone would believe me. I dreamt a tiny little baby, like an embryo, was all bloody and crawling up my stomach to nurse. In my dream I was thinking, "No, baby, you're too little. It's not time. It's not time." I woke up and tried to dismiss the dream.

At school during lunch I went in to the school minister's office and just cried hysterically. I really did think my world fell apart. Everything was wrong and I deserved it. I had to leave that very day. I was shaking when I left lesson plans for the sub and I swear there were tearstains on the paper. I didn't care. I was leaving anyway. I was in no shape to drive. My husband left work to come to pick me up from school . . . when he drove me to the ob-gyn he was still hopeful. He said, "Maybe we will just get to see the baby early." I said, "No." It's already gone. I knew it. I wasn't being negative. I knew Buddha [her nickname for her unborn baby] was gone and God himself had left me. I was ashamed and broken. I felt like my body had betrayed me and I had let everyone down.

Many women learn of their unborn child's death in the doctor's office, and the way that medical personnel respond can affect their experience significantly, for better or for worse. Often, women need or elect to have a D&C procedure (dilation and curettage, a surgery usually done under general anesthesia in which the cervix is dilated and all remaining tissue from the pregnancy is scraped from the uterus). Some women discover that the baby has stopped growing or has died, and they have to decide whether to have the D&C right away or to wait until their bodies figure out that the baby is no longer living. Susan shared what this was like for her:

I thought the pregnancy was normal. The only difference I had felt was that I hadn't been as nauseous, but I just figured that was because I was getting close to the end of my first trimester; I was about eleven weeks. We went in for our checkup. Dr. Bissell put the wand (like there is magic in it) on my belly. Nothing. Again. Nothing. She said something like, "Let's go do an ultrasound. Sometimes they're just hiding." We walked down the hallway to the ultrasound room.

Thankfully, Matt [her husband] was with me. She began the ultrasound. I knew. There was nothing. Just stillness. I immediately started to sob. I don't even know where it came from. I think Matt was in shock. "Well, damn," was what Dr. Bissell said. Looking back, I'm grateful for that kind of response. I wouldn't have wanted some sort of scientific explanation.

One of the hardest things about the type of miscarriage I had was that since my body hadn't eliminated (awful term, but I can't think of a better one) the fetus, we had to decide what we wanted to do: wait and see, take some sort of drug that would allow my body to deliver, or a D&C. We went home, thought about our options, which of course once the shock wears off only spurs more questions. We met the next Monday at the doctor's office and, after some more conversation, decided on the D&C. You would think that would be it, but I didn't realize that we had to schedule an operating room, which meant that it would be two more days before the procedure could be done. I remember once we had decided on the operation, I just wanted it out. I hated going around with a dead baby (crude, but true) inside of me.

Some women have just days between the positive pregnancy test and the miscarriage that poses as a late period. Some women have pregnancies that seem fine until the tenth or eleventh week. Some women have pregnancies that keep them teetering on that fine edge between fear and hope for months, with occasional bleeding, funny physical symptoms, or a nagging feeling that something just isn't right. And some women grieve instantly, while others feel guilty at the smothered relief that floods them.

The experience of miscarriage can be complicated further by the feelings of guilt that can immediately rush in. This was a difficult part of Christine's experience:

> Pregnancy #1 was a miscarriage in week eleven. I felt broken and actually felt it was punishment for an elective abortion I had at the age of seventeen. Although I believed strongly in God, my spiritual upbringing taught me that God punished us for our sins. A family member who had taken me to the emergency room overheard a nurse complain about having to clean up my private area, and so I felt humiliated and a burden. I had to have a D&C because they told me they needed to remove the rest of the "tissue." There was no social worker or chaplain. As I awoke from anesthesia, I found myself in a room with a woman who had had a hysterectomy, and I was discharged before I could even stand.

This guilt can be related to something concrete, as it was for Christine (a previous abortion, smoking or drinking during the first part of the pregnancy— even though most of these things are unlikely to have caused the miscarriage) or to something abstract (the worry that you were not praying enough, that you were not happy enough about the pregnancy, that you were not going to be a good enough mother). In nearly all these cases, the guilt is related to the grief of the loss rather than to anything that would have affected the pregnancy. However, that fact doesn't usually make it any easier to let go of such feelings of guilt.

Women who have been struggling with infertility can have particularly complicated emotions. Even more so than with other women, less-fertile women's pregnancies might seem all the more precious because they have been so long in coming. When she lost her first pregnancy after nine years of infertility challenges, Heather said:

> We saw a heartbeat on two different ultrasounds, but when we went back for our eleven-week ultrasound, the baby had died. I was devastated. I didn't know that a baby's heart could stop beating. We scheduled a D&C for the next morning. The doctor was nice but kept calling it a "fluke." The whole evening before the D&C I wept constantly . . . I cried all through the check-in process at the hospital the next morning. When a nurse said, "You can try again," I told her she didn't understand . . . it had taken me nine years to get pregnant with this one.

Your pregnancy loss may have been very different from your best friend's. Your experience at the doctor's office may have felt cold and impersonal, while your sister experienced only compassion from medical personnel. Your physical experience may have been the most traumatic part of your loss, while for your co-worker the emotional impact was stronger. There is no "right" way to feel, no "right" way for you to respond to your miscarriage. But in every case, the miscarriage brings a tragic full stop to the hope and excitement and fear of pregnancy.

REFLECTION QUESTIONS

1. Reflect on your experience of miscarriage. Tell your own story. Did you anticipate the loss? Did it come out of the blue? Who was with you? When did you know?
2. Think about your experience with medical professionals. Were they helpful? Hurtful? How did they make you feel?

EXERCISE

Find art supplies you are comfortable using (paper and paints, pastels or crayons, modeling clay, or something else) and use them to express your experience of your miscarriage. When you are finished, share your artwork with a trusted person and explain it to her or him.

Chapter 3

The Days After

*C*hris and I drove the miles back to our home in Blacksburg much more slowly than we had covered them on the way to the hospital. There was nothing to hurry for. Familiar milestones along the interstate clicked by: the bright yellow outlet mall in Gaffney, the enormous water tower shaped and painted like an extraterrestrial peach, the church that had set up in an old shopping center and put a sign on the marquee that said, "The Rapture: Don't Miss It!" I felt dull and empty. There was an unbearable sameness to the road. All the comfortable markings that were supposed to lead us home seemed callous and dingy, impermeable to our great loss. I would see something that would trigger a normal train of thought, and I'd forget for a moment, forget that I was no longer pregnant, and then, just as suddenly, the weight of grief would rush in and settle heavily back in our car.

Our parsonage was no better. The side door had always seemed like a refuge to me, the entrance to the home warmed by our marriage, enfolded by love and comfort and security. That day I noticed the wear on the stoop, irritably aware of the dented bend in the handrail and the mess of books and papers I'd left just inside the door. The four-bedroom house seemed ludicrously big for two people, and it smelled musty, as if we'd been gone for months. Every room bore the mark of my dreams for the lost little one, the baby who would never snuggle by the fire, never sleep in the bedroom, never spill food on the kitchen floor.

And oh, God, how I ached. Every time I went into the bathroom, clotted blood poured from my womb, and I tortured myself examining the clots to see if one looked like it might contain an embryo. I hated my body. It had betrayed me unforgivably. I would have done anything to protect, to shield this little life. I *had* done all the right things. I would have put my body between my baby's body and fire or flood or any sort of danger. And yet my body—the same body I would have given without thought to save this

21

baby—*my* body had been the means of (his? her?) death. Oh, I knew that the doctor had said it wasn't my fault. But there I was with my contracting uterus and no child, and the blame had to settle somewhere. I remember stumbling out of the bathroom in tears, grabbing the towel bar, and trying to punch myself in the stomach. I suddenly realized the complete absurdity of what I was doing. At the same time, it was as if my self-understanding as a being with separate body and self merged back together, and I was washed with a wave of intense pity for my poor, bleeding, hurting body/self. I hugged my abdomen, as if to apologize, and sank onto the floor to cry. There had to be some punishment; there had to be a guilty party. And I was the closest scapegoat available.

Where nonspecific guilt ran up against its limits, pseudoscientific guilt took over. After all, those pregnancy books all prescribed such careful diets. I had been doing my best, I really had, but there had been some days when I didn't get all the vitamins I was supposed to have. Could all that time in the car have hurt the baby? I didn't get out every hour to stretch my legs like the book had recommended; was it a circulation problem? Did I walk too much, or not enough? We had feral cats running around the neighborhood; had I unintentionally made contact with cat feces? I pored over the pregnancy book I had, looking at every suggestion, wild with fear that I'd missed something that had seemed trivial that had cost my baby its life. My mother, my husband, everyone told me that it hadn't been anything I'd done, but the gnawing guilt was relentless. Because really, I was the only one who'd had contact with the baby. And if all these tiny changes in diet and habits were important enough to list in books and on Web sites, surely they were important enough to affect the mysterious changes happening in the darkness of my womb.

To this guilt was soon added another kind of guilt—that I was overreacting horribly. Why couldn't I just pull myself together? *It was still so early*, I lectured myself. *It's not like you even knew the child yet. Just think about people with* real *grief to bear*, I chided. *People in developing countries who expect to lose their children—their real, born children. People who lose infants or three-year-olds. People who lose their whole families in genocides or fires or famine. You've really got to just suck it up. I'm disappointed in you*, I concluded. *You must be incredibly weak.*

I had intended to go back up to school for class on Tuesday, with that "stiff upper lip" lecture at the fore. But after I spent Monday drifting around the house, hurting terribly, and uninterested in anything beyond mulling over my loss, Chris encouraged me to take a week off, and I decided that he was right. I told myself that it was because of the drive and my physical condition. I e-mailed my professors and settled in for a week of licking my wounds.

The week slipped by in a fog of tears and pain. And God? God I mostly ignored. There was this huge, weighty sense of anger and betrayal and disbelief rumbling around at the edges of my conscious mind, but I couldn't even begin to let it in. I wanted to pray, wanted to feel connected to the steadfast God I had loved and known and tried to follow, but I felt about God as I'd imagine feeling about my spouse if he were to have an affair—our whole history of relationship, our whole journey together, the collected life of brilliant moments of intimacy and plodding months of growth was called into question. *Who are you, anyway?* I wanted to shout. *I don't even know you anymore!* The only way I could find voice to pray was in music. I would sit at our glossy black piano, my husband's engagement gift to me, and morosely finger chords. I would open the hymnal at least once a day and play through other people's prayers: Martin Luther's "Out of the Depths I Cry to You," "Be Still, My Soul," Dietrich Bonhoeffer's "By Gracious Powers." I could trace my way through their prayers, and the music gave my voice a channel, at least for those few moments. And using other Christians' words, written by Christians who had known deep, profound, legitimate suffering, allowed me to mouth words of hope, even when they felt like farce. Still, I made Chris promise to keep our loss a secret from the members of his churches. I didn't want stilted sympathy or awkward conversations. And I determined I'd go to church the following Sunday as if nothing had happened.

We decided I needed to get out of the house, so Chris and I drove back to Spartanburg to see the free foreign film series at Wofford College. They were showing *Y tu mamá tambien.* I sat in the tiered classroom, looking at the impossibly young undergraduates. I was barely three years older than many of them, but felt separated by a chasm of loss. I remember heading to the bathroom halfway through the movie, lugging my purse stuffed with its "supplies," walking awkwardly around the heavy pad, resting my head on my hands in the stall. The whole week seemed to consist of moments of misery in anonymous restrooms, strung together on a misty cord of unreality. In which toilet, which sewer system, was our child buried now?

I knew that our extended family wanted to help. My parents, far away in Indiana, mourned that they were not close enough to hug me. Both Chris's and my parents and other family members called and said loving things, but I felt disconnected from them as well. I was floating in a strange bubble that contained all my pain, and when anyone but Chris got too close to the perimeter, it threatened to burst and flood me. Distance was necessary.

Every night, I cried myself to sleep, burrowing fiercely into my husband's side or tunneling under the covers, trying to hide from the grief, whispering over and over, "I want my baby—oh *God,* I want my baby."

Thus it was that when I returned to Durham the next Tuesday, I had a surreal sense of having lived through a nightmare that wasn't connected to anyone else's reality. We had not told many people that I was pregnant, "just in case something happens," although I had no idea that "something" would actually happen, and no concept of what that "something" would feel like. The result of this, of course, was that no one knew. Few even noticed I'd been gone—I was sort of a commuter, after all—and my friends and acquaintances greeted me with normal cheer.

Halfway through my first class, I found myself battling a strange impulse to stand up and scream out, "I had a miscarriage last week, and I am bleeding and broken and miserable! For God's sake, someone tell me that you care!" Instead of doing that, I started awkwardly shoving the news into unrelated conversations. "Hey, how are you?" a friend would ask. Instead of the expected, "Fine, thanks, and how was your weekend?" I would say, "I'm terribly sad. I didn't tell you, but I was pregnant, and I had a miscarriage last week." Of course this had the effect of a rough slap to the face. People would stop dead, focus on me, and then I could almost see them gathering the shreds of Pastoral Care 101 around them. I would immediately feel guilty for violating some perceived academic social contract and for not being able to keep my grief to myself.

At worship the next day, I nearly had a public meltdown. I had gone grudgingly; I had never missed a regular worship service for any reason besides illness or vacation, and I wanted to meet God, to see if God would dare to show God's face, to see if God had anything to say to me. The worship that day was an exuberant praise service. Had I been in a sunny mood, it would have been a delight. But everything sounded sarcastic to me. "The Lord delivers the righteous!" *Oh great, I thought, so I'm unrighteous? That's why you killed my baby?* "Shout to the Lord!" *Shout what? "I hate you?"* "God has counted the hairs on your head!" That was the point at which I could take no more. I waited as long as I could, but when the choir burst into clapping and song, and everyone around me was clapping and singing and smiling, tears erupted from my eyes and I roughly shoved my way down the row of chairs and escaped through the library door. I fled to the Women's Center, a small room off the hallway outside the student lounge. It was set up to allow breastfeeding, but there was a small altar and a bookshelf full of worship resources, and I collapsed there and cried until I was empty.

WHAT MAY HAPPEN PHYSICALLY

Every woman's body is different, and every miscarriage is different, but here are some things other women have experienced during the first days and weeks after the miscarriage.

Your doctor will almost certainly offer three options (although for some women one option may be strongly recommended over another): (1) allow your body to complete the miscarriage on its own; (2) take medications to assist your body to complete the miscarriage; (3) have a D&C (dilation and curettage, a surgery in which the cervix is dilated and the uterus is scraped clean). No matter which option you choose, miscarriage will be a painful experience; there is no "magic bullet" that can make it pleasant. Studies have shown little difference in the grief response among the three methods. Here are some of the benefits and challenges some women have experienced with each of these options.

If you choose to allow your body to complete the miscarriage without a D&C, you can expect to bleed for well over a week (and up to three) as your body expels the pregnancy and the supply of blood and uterine lining that had built up to nourish it. Depending on how advanced your pregnancy was, this can feel similar to an extremely heavy period, or it can feel much, much more intense. Megan was surprised by "just how much miscarrying is like real labor (if you don't have a D&C). Especially if you are farther along. And in some ways I think that it is more painful . . . because there is *no joy* in it. All that pain for what? A dead baby in your toilet?"

If you are miscarrying without surgery, often painkillers like ibuprofen or naproxen sodium can help reduce the cramps, especially after the first several days. You will not be allowed to use tampons (because of the risk of infection), so you will see a great deal of blood and clots as the uterine lining and pregnancy pass from your body. Depending on how far along your pregnancy is, you may or may not notice or be able to tell when your baby and/or placenta are passed. Some women who can tell find this an incredibly painful experience; some are relieved to be able to keep the baby's body from being flushed down the toilet. Sometimes, your doctor may ask you to save the fetus so that genetic testing can be done to determine whether the miscarriage happened because of a developmental problem with the baby or because of another kind of problem. Such testing is more common when a woman has experienced multiple miscarriages and a treatable factor is more likely in play. If your doctor knows you are miscarrying and thinks that this information would be valuable, she or he may encourage a D&C precisely because it is much more likely that testing and evaluation will yield useful information on a fetus that is removed in a sterile and closed environment.

Some women find the extended bleeding of nonsurgical miscarriage very traumatic. Others are relieved to avoid a surgery that they find invasive or frightening. Some women's bodies will not completely empty the uterus. If this happens, the risks of an untreated infection are high, so your doctor will check your hormone levels regularly to make sure the miscarriage is complete. If your body does not complete the miscarriage, you may have to have a D&C in order to prevent a serious uterine infection.

If you do have a D&C procedure, you will not have the same kind of extended bleeding. You will be put to sleep or heavily sedated for the outpatient surgery. Some women are glad to end the process of miscarrying the pregnancy quickly. Other women have trouble with the surgery itself, finding it invasive or frightening. A friend of mine who lost two pregnancies between ten and eleven weeks completed one miscarriage at home and had a D&C for the second. For her personally, it proved to be far less traumatic to have the D&C than to watch the pregnancy bleed away over the extended time. Other women prefer the route that seems more natural to them.

Some pregnancies are advanced far enough that women need to have labor induced and deliver the fetus vaginally. This can be terribly difficult, especially during the time between the diagnosis of fetal death and the induction of labor. The thought of being pregnant with a dead child is profoundly disturbing for almost everyone who experiences it. Many women's bodies are fooled into behaving as if they are still pregnant for days, and so morning sickness or other pregnancy symptoms may continue. These symptoms are unpleasant at any time, but when they are associated with the impending joy of a new baby, they seem worthwhile. To continue to experience nausea and extreme fatigue while knowing your child is dead can be extraordinarily painful. And to go through the experience of labor, the process that is associated with new life, knowing that your labor will bring forth only death, is simply heartbreaking.

If you choose to have a D&C or an induced labor, you will want to talk to your physician ahead of time about what will become of your baby's body. If you are very early, it may not be desirable or even practical to ask to see the fetus, but nonetheless, you should be able to do this if you want to. If your pregnancy is more advanced, especially if you have seen ultrasounds that are recognizably childlike, you will certainly want to talk to the doctor about what will happen to that baby's body.[1] Although it is sometimes discouraged, especially for early losses, it can be very helpful in the long term to take charge of that body yourself, to see and say good-bye to your baby.

Even if you do not choose to see or touch the baby's body, arranging for your baby to be buried or cremated can provide a healing memory in months and years to come.

No matter how the pregnancy ends physically, the weeks after are complicated because of hormone levels as well. As your body stops producing pregnancy hormones and works to regain its nonpregnant state of equilibrium, you will almost certainly notice effects on your mood and emotions. It can be hard to tell sometimes what feelings are related to the grief of the pregnancy loss and what feelings are related to hormone-affected mood changes. Either way, your emotions will almost certainly be a mess. Even after a pregnancy ending with a live child, the thud of dropping hormone levels can trigger baby blues. Women grieving a lost baby can be sent into a tailspin.

WHAT MAY HAPPEN EMOTIONALLY

First, let's repeat what we said earlier: studies have shown that the grief experience after losing a wanted pregnancy, no matter how advanced it is, is very similar to the grief experience after losing a close family member or friend. You can expect to hurt intensely for a time, and then you can expect the pain gradually to get easier to bear. If you can hold on for six months, the pain will be much less intense. If you've ever lost a parent or sibling, this will sound familiar. Here are two important differences:

1. We expect to hurt like this when we lose a loved one. We do not necessarily expect to hurt like this when we have a miscarriage. Therefore, the pain may come as a surprise, and many women feel guilty or abnormal for hurting as much as they do.

2. Friends and family tend to acknowledge the pain associated with the loss of a loved one much more readily. Often, people do not expect, understand, or validate this pain when it is associated with a miscarriage.

Your experience of grief following your miscarriage will in many ways be comparable to other experiences of grief in your life. There are lots of helpful resources for grieving in general, many of which are predicated on the five stages of grief outlined in the classic *On Death and Dying* by Elisabeth Kübler-Ross. Her "stages" are outlined below, along with some examples of how they may appear in your experience of pregnancy loss. Remember that grief is highly personal. Your loss will feel different depending on circumstances in your history, your personality, and your pregnancy. And please note: these stages are neither clearly defined nor even sequential; they might be better described as "characteristics." A person may experience only one or two stages, or all five; a person may go through them one at a time or experience aspects of two or more at the same time, in any order. They are also not consistently experienced at the same intensity; they will fluctuate, becoming more intense some days, ebbing on others, then cycling back into higher intensity again. Although the intensity of your grief experience will wax and wane, the *most* intense period of your grief will usually peak within six months. If it continues getting worse or fails to improve at all after that time, you should seek the help of a skilled counselor.[2]

Denial/Disbelief

This is sometimes the first reaction to your loss. It can be hard to adjust quickly from "I am pregnant; we are having a baby!" to "I am no longer pregnant; we have lost the baby." As part of this reaction to the loss, you may think or say things like, "I can't believe this is happening!" "Do you think the doctors made a mistake?" "I am sure I'm still pregnant! I would know if anything was wrong!" Some women report still feeling pregnant, which is due as much to lingering hormones in the body as it is to any psychological desire to remain pregnant. But because they still feel pregnant and may be experiencing pregnancy symptoms, it can be all the more difficult to accept that the baby has been lost.

Anger

For many women, anger is a major part of their grief response. The anger may be directed at any one of a number of targets. With miscarriage in particular, it is common for anger to be directed toward oneself (in whose body did the loss take place, after all?) or toward God (isn't God supposed to be in charge of these things?). Anger may also be directed toward one's spouse or partner, one's parents, or other friends or acquaintances who respond in ways that feel painful or inappropriate. It is also common for anger to be directed toward other women who are having children, either women who seem to take poor care of their children (particularly those who are on drugs or taking other risks) or women who seem to become pregnant very easily.

This leads directly back to anger at God ("I would be an *infinitely* better parent—how come she can have children and I can't?").

Yearning/Bargaining

Yearning was the grief characteristic I experienced the most strongly, and it seems to be the characteristic most people experience for the longest time after a pregnancy loss. It describes the *feeling* of loss, of missing the pregnancy and the baby. "I want my baby back!" is a common way to express this. Or, "I wish I were still pregnant!" Because the feelings of loss are both strong and close to the surface of your consciousness, anything and everything—pregnant women, small children or babies, baby clothing displays, baby bottles at the grocery store, a park you had thought you'd like to take a child to someday—can remind you of your loss and trigger intense feelings of yearning.

Bargaining is often associated with this stage as well, usually when there seems to be a possibility of a different outcome. During a miscarriage, you might say, "God, if you can stop this from happening, I will be the best mother that's ever lived." "If this baby lives, I will finally start going to church." Bargaining is a natural way of trying to regain some control over the outcome of a painful situation. Some women may fear that their miscarriage is God's way of punishing them for something and may desperately try to avoid the punishment by striking a bargain. We will talk more about this later, but for now, I will just say clearly that miscarriage is *not* God's judgment on you or your baby for anything you have done or not done. The impulse to bargain with God comes from our own pain, not from a desire God has for you to strike a deal with the Divine.

Depression

Depression is not the same thing as sadness. It is an enduring low state of being characterized by several specific symptoms. Common signs of depression include uncontrollable crying, walking around in a fog, ruminating thoughts (thoughts that center around a loss or a component of the loss and cycle over and over), an inability to function normally, and impulsivity (a category that includes things like difficulty sleeping, lack of motivation, an inability to find pleasure in activities or events that you had usually enjoyed, an increase or decrease in eating). Your everyday experiences will usually be seen through the lens of a depressed mood—in other words, everything you see, every conversation you have, filters through your sadness. A depressed person rarely knows she is depressed until she is no longer in this state. You may have to trust your spouse or those around you if they are concerned and see you displaying some of the symptoms. Caring for your body will be important, particularly getting regular exercise, eating a nourishing, balanced selection of foods, and staying on a regular sleep schedule. Unfortunately, the symptoms of depression make it more difficult to care for yourself in all three of these ways. If it is practical, enlist the help of loved ones: ask your husband if he will take a walk with you daily, or ask your mother if she'll help provide meals for a while. Skilled counselors can help you manage and treat your depression if it is keeping you from normal functioning.

Acceptance

You will almost certainly not find your way into a state of acceptance within the first days and weeks following your miscarriage. This will come much farther down the road. "Acceptance" does *not* mean that you will feel good about your loss, or that you will suddenly think that it was a positive event. Instead, "acceptance" in this case describes what happens when you accept that this loss is part of your life and find ways to integrate the loss into your own story. It's the discovery of a new equilibrium after the loss that describes the way your life is going to be from that point onward.

A WORD ABOUT GUILT

The struggle with guilt is especially present in miscarriage. Typically, women seem to experience less guilt when there is an identifiable cause for the miscarriage, but since so many miscarriages are chalked up to unknown causes, this does not help most of us. Feelings of guilt almost always are connected to significant losses (if you've lost a family member, you may recognize this; people often say things like, "I should have spent more time with her" or "I wish I'd written more letters" or "If I'd only come home early from work that day, I could have been there"). Normal feelings of guilt that accompany any loss are ramped up with miscarriage, because the loss happened inside your very body. Not only do most women feel generally guilty, they also feel as if they must have done something specific to cause the miscarriage, even when other people tell them they have not.

These feelings of guilt can also be expressed in relation to God. Many women I've talked to have said, "What did I do wrong? Is God punishing me?" These same women would never imagine that a loss experienced by a friend was a punishment from God; in other words, the association is not rational. But it is natural.

In the film *Good Will Hunting*, therapist Sean Maguire (Robin Williams) is talking to mathematical genius Will (Matt Damon) about the abuse Will received from his stepfather. Sean says to him, "Will, it's not your fault." Will sort of shrugs and smiles and says, "I know." "It's not your fault," Sean repeats. "Yeah, I know," says Will. Sean repeats the phrase, "It's not your fault . . . it's not your fault . . . it's not your fault," battering down the protective layers Will has built over his self-blame for his stepfather's abuse, until Will breaks down, because he can finally allow himself to hear and believe what Sean is saying to him.

I emphatically wish I could say the same to you. It's not your fault. It's *not* your fault. God is not punishing you; this did not happen because of anything you did or didn't do; it's not your fault. The aftermath of miscarriage will take you on a painful ride, full of unexpected emotions, unfamiliar reactions, uncharted territory of the body and spirit. Be gentle with yourself. Allow yourself to seek the help you need to move from one day into the next. Give yourself grace when you cry more than you think you should, when you lash out in anger, when you can't seem to get off the couch or out of your pajamas. And know that whether you can sense God's presence or not, God is with you—loving you, hurting for you, holding you in steadfast love.

REFLECTION QUESTIONS

1. Think about the days and weeks following your own miscarriage. What was it like? If you are living through it now, how do you feel?
2. During the time directly following your miscarriage, how do you wish people had cared for you? If you are grieving now, what would help? Is there someone you can ask for this kind of care?

EXERCISE

Draw a picture that represents you experiencing your miscarriage. If you are comfortable doing so, share your picture with someone you trust.

Chapter 4

The Medical Basics of Miscarriage

As I wandered through the days and weeks after the miscarriage, a recurring question wove through my thoughts: why had this happened? Was there something wrong with the baby's development, some cellular misstep that mushroomed as the cells divided? I remembered sitting down with the divinity school chaplain weeks before, telling her that according to a Web site I'd seen, the baby was on that very day the size of a grain of rice. She had seized a piece of scrap paper and a pen and carefully drawn a life-sized grain of rice as we looked at it and laughed incredulously. Plenty could go wrong inside something the size of a grain of rice.

Conception in itself is a sort of miracle. When I looked at all the against-the-odds things that have to click into place for pregnancy to occur, I marveled that the human race has been propagated for so long. One healthy egg has to be properly matured and released, one healthy sperm has to make its way to the egg in a window of hours, the zygote has to find a nourishing place to attach within the uterus . . . and then the real development begins. The statistical odds against getting to this point are enormous. If there is a tiny genetic abnormality in the sperm or egg, if the codes held within the two happen to interact poorly, the growing life may quickly become biologically unsustainable. The surprising thing, then, is not that there are so many miscarriages, but that there are any healthy babies born at all, to anyone. So maybe that had been the problem. Maybe, as so many people kept reassuring me, nature had "solved a problem" on its own.

Then again, maybe there was another reason, I brooded—a reason located not in a crummy roll of the dice, but within my own body. Perhaps my uterus was shaped poorly for carrying children, or perhaps my hormones were out of balance. What if I *had* eaten or touched something that was poisonous for the nascent life within me, or had done something that affected my body and therefore my baby's unborn, unformed body? What if having sex while pregnant really *was* a problem, despite assurances to the contrary in the baby book? What if there was a pill I could have taken, an activity I could have changed, to save my baby's life? Or, perhaps worst of all, what if there was something wrong with me that would never allow me to have children? What if we kept getting pregnant and losing pregnancies, over and over, forever?

These fears were not unique to me, and the normal guilt that accompanies a loss causes most women to dwell on these questions far beyond the point that their intellect knows is appropriate. Jana remembered, "The morning of my miscarriage, I had swept and washed the first-floor hardwood floors. I went over that action many times in my mind in the weeks that followed, wondering if I had inadvertently caused the miscarriage, then chastising myself for imagining that, then guiltily wondering it yet again." In such cases, be gentle with yourself, and realize that the medical answers are probably not going to give you immediate peace. I had read in at least five trustworthy sources that having sex or climbing stairs could not cause miscarriage, and yet I kept wondering, kept Googling.

Some women can talk to their doctors and receive sufficient information to calm their concerns. Other women handle their grief and uncertainty by researching the questions, sometimes obsessively (speaking from personal experience here). It can be helpful for all women, however, to have some basic medical facts about miscarriage. After reading this section, you will *not* be able to "diagnose" yourself, to figure out why your own miscarriage happened. I am a pastor, not a medical professional—you will need to talk to your own doctor to receive expert medical information. But I will share with you some general statistics and information, so that you can see what medical experts know about these losses. If you want more details, please see chapter 14 for resources. (Again, I strongly recommend that if you want more information, you talk to your doctor and perhaps select a trustworthy book rather than doing endless and unverified Internet research.) Most of the following information is applicable to pregnancies that end before fourteen weeks. Second-trimester miscarriages are much rarer and the diagnosis will be somewhat different.

Most doctors do not begin to do testing related to pregnancy loss until after two or three consecutive losses. This can be extremely frustrating for a woman who has just miscarried, so it's important to know why this is typical medical practice. In most first-trimester pregnancy losses, the loss is due to reproductive errors that are not likely to recur. Doctors do not want to inflict unnecessary testing on patients, and for half of women who have had their first miscarriage, testing would cost a great deal of money and reveal nothing about the cause of the miscarriage. That said, you are certainly permitted to ask your doctor to perform testing. Keep in mind, however, that many of these tests have a 1 to 2 percent chance of yielding information. Nonconclusive data from tests has been known to result in unnecessary treatments in future pregnancies, treatments that carry some risks. This is why doctors do not recommend these tests until there is a stronger clinical reason (two or three losses with no live births) to suggest a treatable disorder.

Testing can potentially be done on the baby's body or the placenta to tell whether the miscarriage was related to chromosomal abnormalities or improper placental formation. However, the yield from chromosomal analysis is often poor. The placenta, while it is usually normal, is more likely to be successfully analyzed. Again, this kind of testing is not usually indicated except with recurrent losses. If you have had recurrent losses, your medical-care provider may ask you to try to save your baby's body and placenta, or any large clots. Both logistically and emotionally, this may be painful for you. It is hard to imagine retrieving from the toilet or saving from the pad the partially formed body of your child. But if having answers about the cause of your miscarriage would be healing for you (and this is, in fact, healing for many women), it can be a very good thing to attempt to do. You can use a clean glass jar (like a Mason jar) or a clean plastic storage container. Know up front that it is hard for most people who are early in their pregnancies to be able to identify their baby. Often, what you collect may not be suitable for analysis. Some patients will collect tissue only to be told that it is clotting or part of the uterine lining, and not their baby at all. If your pregnancy is more advanced, on the other hand, you may be able to recognize the fetus and placenta. It may help you to be able to treat that tiny body with respect and care. You could choose a special scarf or handkerchief to wrap around the container for your trip to the office or lab, and you could say prayers or have a brief family service commemorating the life of your child before taking the container in. (Some examples of such prayers are found in chapter 14.)

WHAT DOES NOT CAUSE MISCARRIAGE

Many women, including myself, bear an amalgam of questionable information about miscarriage swirling in their brains, made up of scraps of half-remembered conversations, sentences read on Web sites, studies reviewed in the newspaper, and old folktales. Therefore, it is worth looking at some common misconceptions and fears about the causes of miscarriage.

Normal Exercise

Normal exercise, including housework, does not cause miscarriage. This fear haunts many women, but this is an old folktale that grew out of the days when the pregnant woman was supposed to be in a "delicate" condition, prone to fainting (never mind the corsets constricting her lungs) and in need of constant rest. While starting an intense, high-impact exercise regimen is not recommended while you are pregnant, regular exercise can actually help protect your pregnancy by keeping you healthy.

Sexual Activity

This is a source of quiet guilt for many women and their partners. Sex during pregnancy is a funny enterprise, running the gamut from incredibly awkward to completely unappealing to more exciting than it's ever been before. Much of the insecurity of the first few times may return, especially during a first pregnancy when the awareness of the presence of a third person suddenly permeates the couple's bed. But regular sexual activity does not cause miscarriage. Semen does contain prostoglandins, which have been associated with triggering uterine contractions, especially late in the pregnancy. But prostoglandins have *never* been shown to cause miscarriage. Sex did not cause you to lose your baby.[1]

A Not-Quite-Perfect Diet

You had a diet soda when you got up in the morning. You didn't eat any green leafy vegetables for almost a week. You had two drinks at a party three days before you did the pregnancy test. You lived on soda crackers, Cheerios, and ginger ale for a solid month because of the nausea. Whatever the dietary challenges you've had, it is highly unlikely that an imperfect pregnancy diet caused your miscarriage (the exceptions would be alcohol drunk regularly or in large quantities, unpasteurized food that caused you to get sick, or possibly coffee in greater quantity than two cups per day). Of course we all want to give our babies the absolute best start, and so those recommended diets handed out at the ob-gyn's office or reproduced on pregnancy sites and in pregnancy books are helpful guides. What you do or do not eat can indeed have an effect on the health of your pregnancy. But please don't take unrealistic guilt on yourself—babies are born every day to highly malnourished women around the globe. The things you did or didn't eat are not likely to have anything to do with your miscarriage.

Stress

When there is no apparent reason for a miscarriage, it can be tempting to chalk it up to stress. "Stress" is a catchall category that seems to cover a wide range of life circumstances. Many of us anecdotally link periods of stress and anxiety in our lives with increased illness, trouble sleeping or eating, headaches, or other physical problems. However, there is absolutely no research-based evidence that indicates that high levels of stress cause miscarriage. In *Miscarriage, Medicine, and Miracles,* Bruce Young and Amy Zavatto point out that "military women returning from Vietnam and Iraq with post-traumatic stress disorder, and civilians in New York City after the horror of September 11, 2001, did not experience a higher miscarriage rate than usual."[2] Stress can and does affect you in myriad ways, and it needs to be dealt with. But there is no reason to think that stress causes miscarriage.

Trips and Falls

When you're pregnant, even before your center of gravity really starts shifting, you may be clumsier or more distracted than usual. Stumbles and tumbles can happen to anyone. But your baby is extraordinarily well protected in your womb, insulated by your own body, by cushiony layers of fluid and flesh. Extremely traumatic physical events, like severe automobile accidents or intense physical abuse, do have the potential to cause miscarriage. But normal trips, tumbles onto the sidewalk, falls onto the floor—even the ones that leave you bruised and aching—are extremely unlikely to cause a miscarriage.

Lifting Heavy Objects

I'll never forget the day I was clearing the table during pregnancy, holding a gallon of milk in each hand, when a well-meaning family member shouted out to me, "Hey, don't carry all that! You're pregnant!!" I laughed at the time, but more than once after my first miscarriage I flipped through my file of memories, wondering if I'd carried something too heavy. Many women who have older children at home feel guilty because they lifted and carried their older children while pregnant, and they fear that caring for their older children caused their pregnancy to end. While excessively strenuous, heavy lifting (moving a piano, for example) is not recommended during any part of pregnancy, normal lifting (groceries, children, one end of the sofa) will not cause a miscarriage. The greater risk is to your own back.

WHY MISCARRIAGES OCCUR

Most miscarriages—perhaps 50 to 60 percent—are due to genetic abnormalities in the fetus. This can happen to any two cells that are combining to form a new life, and it usually has no determinable cause. Sometimes that particular egg had not fully matured or was overmature or otherwise unhealthy; sometimes that particular sperm was deformed or damaged; sometimes in the combination of the two, DNA replicated improperly. If this was the reason for your miscarriage, there is nothing you could have done to prevent it. These errors occurred before you even realized you were pregnant.

Other miscarriages are caused by some other factor. You will need to talk to your doctor and perhaps begin testing to determine if one of these causes contributed to your own miscarriage or miscarriages. Some of the more common nongenetic reasons for miscarriage are listed below. Making choices about treatment for any of these conditions or concerns is never a one-size-fits-all proposition. Developing a good relationship with a trusted medical-care provider is essential.

Infection or Illness

Sometimes an infection or illness in the mother's system can cause miscarriage. These can be divided into three groups: (1) chronic medical conditions, such as thyroid disease, diabetes, or autoimmune disorders (in these cases, medical management prior to becoming pregnant can optimize the chance of a good outcome); (2) one-time illnesses like rubella, fifth disease (parvovirus), toxoplasmosis CMV, or even the flu with a high fever (these causes are unlikely to recur because of lasting immunities developed by your body); and (3) other diseases or infections, such as syphilis and vaginal infections (these can be treated and eliminated from the mother's body).

Hormone Imbalances

A woman's reproductive cycle is a beautifully balanced ebb and flow of the release of various hormones. If either too little or too much of a certain hormone is produced, or if a hormone is produced for an insufficient amount of time, it can affect various parts of that cycle. Ovulation, the release of the egg, can be affected both in timing and in maturity of the egg; the process of implantation, in which the fertilized egg attaches to the uterine lining, is affected by hormones; and the buildup of the lining itself is dependent on the flux of hormones in the woman's body. One concern with hormone production is the length of time that progesterone is produced after the egg has been released. If progesterone levels are too low or available for an insufficient amount of time, the egg may fail to attach securely to the uterine wall. Some doctors may prescribe progesterone supplements (often in suppository form), although the research on how effective this is has been inconclusive and the potential risks in the long term may outweigh possible benefits. This can be challenging to sort out, because low progesterone levels can be a symptom of a failing pregnancy rather than the cause. Your doctor will be able to look at your own cycle and help you make appropriate decisions given your circumstances.

Cervical Insufficiency

Unfortunately, this condition is also called "incompetent" cervix. It usually does not affect pregnancies until the second trimester, typically after the fourth month. As the baby grows, an insufficient cervix may open prematurely and allow a miscarriage between the thirteenth and twentieth weeks (later losses are termed stillbirths). Once your health-care professional is aware of this issue, it usually can be treated with a procedure called cerclage, in which a stitch is placed around the cervix to help support the weight of the pregnancy. These are typically placed at the beginning of the second trimester.

Septate Uterus

This refers to a congenital problem with the woman's uterus, in which a band of tissue (septum) runs down the center of her uterus and divides it. It can be a factor in repeated miscarriages. Surgery to remove the band of tissue is the primary treatment, and it can greatly increase your probability of being able to carry a pregnancy to term. There are many variations on this, and what type of surgical correction is best and when it ought to take place must be determined individually.

Uterine Fibroids

Fibroids are benign muscle masses that occur in the uterine wall. The primary study done on uterine fibroids and miscarriage indicated that there is a correlation between the two, and that smaller fibroids are more likely than larger ones to be connected to pregnancy loss. Because not all fibroids cause symptoms that a woman notices, she may be unaware that she has them at all, although they are very common. Many women have fibroids that do not cause problems with their pregnancies.

Ultrasound imaging is used to diagnose fibroids, and pharmacological and occasionally surgical treatments are available. Most fibroids do not need to be surgically removed. Surgery has the potential to damage the uterus or fallopian tubes, which creates difficulty with future pregnancies. Fibroids that protrude into the uterine cavity are the ones that are most often considered for surgical removal.

SPECIAL PREGNANCIES

Finally, there are some special pregnancies that cannot be sustained for quite specific reasons. These pregnancy losses may lead to specific sorts of emotional concerns later, and so we'll address them separately.

Ectopic (Usually Tubal) Pregnancy

Ectopic pregnancy occurs when a fertilized egg implants in a part of the woman's body outside the uterus. You may have seen a bizarre version of this on the season 5 premiere of the medical drama *House*, in which a fetus attached to a woman's large intestine. Although this particular scenario is possible, it is quite rare. More commonly, ectopic pregnancies ("ectopic," by the way, basically means "out of place") implant in the fallopian tubes, sometimes because endometrial or other tubal scarring keeps the fertilized egg from traveling the rest of the way into the uterus, sometimes for no apparent reason at all. This is called a tubal pregnancy. Ectopic pregnancy is rare, accounting for about 2 percent of all reported pregnancies, but is becoming more common. It is extremely dangerous to the mother, since as the fetus grows it eventually will rupture the organ in which it has implanted (usually the fallopian tubes) and cause serious internal bleeding.

Women with ectopic pregnancies will have to have the pregnancy removed. Some may be able to be treated medically; many will have to have surgery. All ectopically attached fetuses will die when the organ ruptures; there is no way to save the baby, nor is it possible to transplant the pregnancy to the correct location. Medical intervention is necessary to save the life of the mother. Some women may find that their feelings of guilt are intensified after such intervention. Some husbands may be much more shaken by the danger to their spouse than by the loss of the pregnancy, and may find that they fear subsequent attempts to become pregnant. Women who have had one ectopic pregnancy should be evaluated as soon as they know they are pregnant again and followed closely until the pregnancy can be clearly seen in the uterus.

Molar Pregnancy

Molar pregnancy is a rare condition in which the placenta develops a mass of cysts (called a mole), and the embryo either does not form at all or forms abnormally.[3] Occasionally, the abnormally ramped-up cell division can continue to the point that precancerous or even cancerous cells form, and the mole itself can become a tumor. Immediate surgical intervention is necessary to remove the molar tissue, and follow-up attention is important to make sure that all of the abnormal tissue has been completely removed and that no cancerous cells recur or spread to other areas in the mother's body. This follow-up should last for six to twelve months. If molar tissue spreads or persists, then the mother will be treated for cancer. Usually these treatments are successful. It is important not to conceive again until it is certain that the molar tissue has not recurred.

Multiple Pregnancy

Pregnancy with multiples is becoming more common in these days of accessible fertility treatments, including the widespread use of Clomid (which stimulates ovulation and may cause more than one egg to be released) and in vitro fertilization (IVF; usually multiple embryos are implanted, and sometimes more than one will successfully attach to the uterine lining and begin growing). It is possible to miscarry all multiples in a pregnancy, and it is also possible to miscarry one or more multiples while one or more survive.

One type of multiple loss is known commonly as vanishing twin syndrome. Imagine this: A woman goes in for an ultrasound and two fetuses are visible on the screen. She and her partner realize that they are having twins. They start making plans, spread the news. Then perhaps she has some spotting, or just goes in for her next appointment or ultrasound, and there is only one heartbeat, or only one baby on the screen. The other twin has "vanished." What has happened in this circumstance is that one of the babies has died, and the fetal tissue has been absorbed. Usually, the living twin will survive and go on to a successful singleton birth.

Parents who experience vanishing twin syndrome, or parents who lose one or more multiples while other multiples in the pregnancy survive, may feel a strange combination of emotions: grief over the lost baby or babies, relief and joy about the baby or babies who survive, guilt because of such relief, or, what is very common, guilt because of the initial feelings of shock they had when they found out that they would be expecting two babies when they had planned for only one. Then parents can expect the whole additional range of complicated emotions associated with miscarriage. Other people may be even more likely to misunderstand or discount the grief of the parents, failing to understand why they can't "just be grateful for what they have." (Please see chapter 11 for an extended discussion of handling conversations about your loss with other people.)

This chapter is not intended to help you self-diagnose. When it comes to the care of bodies, there is absolutely no substitute for the work of a well-trained, intelligent, careful medical professional who is experienced in the diagnosis and treatment of pregnancy loss. And by the by, there *is* such a thing as too much time spent on the Internet, lingering in diagnostic chat rooms, combing through strangely translated Web sites looking for the little-known reason that you lost your baby. It is common for grieving people to respond this way, but it is likely to focus your grief in unhelpful places. Information overload is stressful, and a relationship with a trusted doctor can provide for your medical needs and questions. It is important, however, that you do trust your doctor. If your doctor's response to your miscarriage has felt uncaring or dismissive, or if you are uncomfortable with the care you are receiving, you may find another doctor. If you would like a fresh look at your situation, then another good option is to ask for a consultation with an ob-gyn who specializes in pregnancies, such as a maternal-fetal-medicine specialist or a reproductive specialist. The advantage to this path is that your doctor is likely to guide you to the best resources in your area, rather than you gambling on which name in the phone book looks the best.

Our bodies are delicate, complex organisms. Your body is unlike any other, and your pregnancy loss is commensurately unique. Some miscarriages can be traced to specific causes, some treatable, some not. The cause of other miscarriages remains a mystery. But no matter the cause, the loss remains real. The grief remains potent. And you will need to be cared for, both physically and otherwise.

REFLECTION QUESTIONS

1. Did you discover a biological reason for your miscarriage? If so, do you think it helped you with your grief? Why or why not? If you did not find a reason, did that affect the intensity of your grief? Why or why not?
2. Reflect on your relationship with your physician or other care provider. What parts of that relationship have been helpful, if any? What parts have not been helpful, if any?

EXERCISE

Take a walk in your neighborhood, a park, or some other place you typically enjoy visiting. As you walk, pay attention to your body: the interplay of mind and muscle, the sensations on your skin, the smells and sights and sounds interpreted by your senses. Spend some time reflecting with God about the lost body of your baby. (Anger, regret, questioning, relief—all of these emotions and more might be appropriate.)

PART 2　　　　　　　The Journey with God

Chapter 5

Why Did God Let This Happen?

Several women have told me that the medical answers were enough for them. "My doctor told me that miscarriage was nature's way of taking care of a pregnancy that had gone terribly wrong," one said. "He told me that we really wouldn't have wanted this pregnancy to develop any further . . . that was incredibly comforting to me." This can, in fact, be a profound solace, resolving some of the guilt and allowing a cleaner grief for many women. But for some other women, there are questions yet to be answered. A woman who came to me for pastoral counseling explained, "I just knew the whole three months, I knew that something wasn't right. . . . I kept spotting and my symptoms were just strange. So I prayed to God—I said, 'God, I know something's wrong, and I just want you to know that if this child is going to have special needs, I promise I will take care of her. I still love her and want her, and if you let me try, I promise to welcome her with love and joy, to teach her about your unconditional love.'" Tears filled her eyes as she continued, "And so I had the miscarriage, and I keep wondering—did God think I wasn't serious? Did God think I wasn't going to be a good enough parent for a baby with special needs?"

The complicated questions of cause and effect can haunt you. If God is the one who creates, the one who crafts humans, who dreams up babies, then what do we do with pregnancies that are so improperly formed that they cannot survive? On the other hand, if we chalk up the "mistakes" to nature or biology, then what happens to our claims that God has made us purposefully and carefully, endowing us with particular gifts and particular characteristics?

I found myself paralyzed by these questions. In the heart of a community that was saturated with God-talk, I found myself torn between two impulses. On the one hand, I desired God desperately. I wanted comfort, I wanted assurance, and I wanted to pray, to feel connected to the Maker of all things.

On the other hand, I was horribly suspicious of God. I did not trust this God, the same God I'd followed across the country to seminary, who had apparently allowed (caused?) my pregnancy to end. Because, it seemed to me, there were three options: (a) God didn't care one way or the other about embryonic life; (b) God was powerless to stop the miscarriage, to heal the developing fetus; or (c) God willed the miscarriage to happen. None of these options was comforting.

SCRIPTURE, GOD, AND UNBORN LIFE

I wanted to start at the beginning, and because I was in school, where my only job was to read, write, and talk about God, I wanted to look at these questions objectively, just as if I were doing research for a paper. I didn't realize it as fully as I might have, but I was channeling a great deal of my grief into this project. I took on what seemed to be the easiest question to answer first. Did God care one way or the other about this tiny baby-to-be I'd lost? Did it matter to God? Or was I overreacting—was it silly to imagine that God might care about a seven-week-old fetus when God was dealing with much more tragic losses all over the world at every moment?

I started with Scripture, and I began by searching for places where the Bible mentions life before birth. Almost the first thing I found was Psalm 51:5, "Indeed, I was born guilty, a sinner when my mother conceived me." Sinful from conception? Then, dear God, what was going to happen to this tiny conceptus?

Haunted by this prayer from the Psalms, I started looking for help doing research—although, as I realize now, I longed for help processing my loss, looking for reassurance that despite David's lament in Psalm 51, another chapter would appear in the story about the little life I'd lost.

We had daily services of morning prayer and three chapel services weekly while I was in school. At one of those weekly chapel services, Communion was served. A couple of weeks after I returned to school, I attended chapel and received Communion feeling painfully empty, and afterward I marched up to the altar. The academic dean, a beautiful spirit with spectacles and a shiny bald head and a habit of singing in his office, often stood at the altar after Communion, beaming on all and sundry and handing out the remaining Communion bread in big, sweet chunks as we filed past on our way back to classes. I approached him and spilled out the story of my loss severely, speaking too quickly, trying to pretend that it was all academic. "And I was wondering what Scripture passages you might recommend," I continued, "that make reference to the personhood of the fetus." I remember that he looked at me gravely, and I suddenly felt transparent, felt as though he could see my raw grief and anger, and it irritated me. But he answered as I'd asked, saying, "The Psalms, and of course Jeremiah as well." I nodded curtly and stalked out of the chapel, thinking, "Right, the Psalms, they've certainly been helpful so far. And anyway, those are nothing but prayers, they're not systematic at all!" I wanted a line I could point to that said, "God cares about your baby, and will take care of the child you lost." I wanted Scripture to answer my questions on my terms. But the Scriptures remained interested in telling stories instead—the stories of other people's groping and grasping for God, hearing a word of piercing clarity, and then wandering in exile for decades. The Scriptures didn't tend to create neat little systems to explain how the world works. And just then, I was in the mood for explicit answers, not mystery.

Grudgingly, I turned back to Psalms anyway. And here, in this collection of prayers that have been offered by God's people alone and in community, at home and at worship, over hundreds of years in vastly different circumstances, I found several other references to life in the womb. Yes, there was Psalm 51, but there were also psalms like Psalm 22, which says, "From birth I was cast upon you; from my mother's womb you have been my God" (Ps. 22:10 NIV). The wicked are wayward from the womb (Ps. 58:3), but God knits each person together in the mother's womb (Ps. 139:13). And those who come forth from their mothers' wombs are brought forth by God (Pss. 22:9; 71:6). Despite the unpleasant irony of God knitting together tiny persons in wombs (does God drop stitches?), the writers of the Psalms clearly expressed that God was in some sense involved and interested in life in utero, in the mysterious space between initial creation and bringing forth of new life.

Ultimately, however, it was in scriptural story that I found a word that began to make a difference to me. What I discovered was a word about *vocation*, or calling. We all too often define "vocation" as "my job" or "a career I'd like to have." But the roots of this word are in the Latin *vocare*, or "voice." A voice names us, calls us by our true name, calls us forth to do and be what we were meant to do and be from our life's beginning. The word has historically been used for religious vocations—one might talk about having a vocation to be a priest or a nun—but it has become popular again in recent years, thanks in part to reflections on the nature of modern ministry and books like Rick Warren's *The Purpose-Driven Life*. At its core, however, the word describes the intersection between the Creator's will and the creature's lived identity. God creates and calls us to be a certain one; we learn to listen to that Voice, learn to live into that particular identity.

It is in this place of vocation—God's voice calling creatures to claim their particular identity and their unique place in the work of creation—that I found another scriptural witness to God's interaction with those who live in the confines of the womb. There were various examples. In Genesis, God speaks to Rebekah about the twins she is carrying, and says, "Two nations are in your womb, and two peoples born of you shall be divided; the one shall be stronger than the other, the elder shall serve the younger" (Gen. 25:23). This isn't just fortune-telling; this is God naming womb-babies personally, marking them by their character and their future. Surely, at the very least, this indicates God's knowledge of persons while they are still in the womb.

The prophets, too, had a strong sense of God creating them purposefully and giving them their vocation from the time of their mothers' pregnancies. Isaiah says that God has "formed me in the womb to be his servant, to bring Jacob back to him, and that Israel might be gathered to him" (Isa. 49:5), while Jeremiah quotes God as saying, "Before I formed you in the womb I knew you, and before you were born I consecrated you; I appointed you a prophet to the nations" (Jer. 1:5). Even before sperm and egg had joined to create zygote, God "knew" Jeremiah. Jeremiah, a particular, individual, human being, is known by God and set apart by God before his heart beats for the first time, before his fingers separate or his eyelids blink. Before he has a tongue, he has a vocation to speak God's truth to a jaded, indifferent world. God's goals for us, our "ends," are connected inextricably to our very beginnings.

Finally, and perhaps most powerfully, in my reading of Scripture I realized that those still in the womb are part of God's story in an active way. Prebirth, precognitive little womb-dwellers are active in the story of God's salvation, active in the story of God transforming a fallen world. Remember the story of the pregnant Elizabeth meeting her pregnant cousin Mary?

> In those days Mary set out and went with haste to a Judean town in the hill country, where she entered the house of Zechariah and greeted Elizabeth. When Elizabeth heard Mary's greeting, the child leaped in her womb. And Elizabeth was filled with the Holy Spirit and exclaimed with a loud cry, "Blessed are you among women, and blessed is the fruit of your womb. And why has this happened to me, that the mother of my Lord comes to me? For as soon as I heard the sound of your greeting, the child in my womb leaped for joy." (Luke 1:39–44)

I brooded over this story. A fetus, an unborn child, is one of the very first to recognize the unborn Jesus and to respond with joy. John the Baptist, in utero, before he can think abstractly or speak or clap his hands or nurse, recognizes Mary as the mother of the fetal Christ. Alone in that mysterious bath of amniotic fluid, connected to adult community only by an umbilical cord, surrounded by the muffled sounds of his mother's body and shifting light and shadow, John perceives the presence of Jesus Christ, God in flesh. The two are separated by mere inches of body and clothing as the mothers draw near to one another. How does a fetus know that he is in the presence of the living God—the living God who is self-bound in the body and being of an even younger fetus, contained in the living body of his mother? John knows immediately what hundreds of grown humans have missed—the people pushing by Mary on the street, the friends she has played with, the parents who gave her birth—that he is in the presence of God in fetal flesh. And his joy translates itself to his mother, causing her to pay attention to the coming of the Messiah as well. John is one of the first evangelists, and he declares the good news by leaping in womb waters to say, "Look! There he is!" Even before his birth, John the Baptist is pointing to the Messiah, fulfilling his ultimate vocation.[1]

These prayers, these narratives, these events underscore that even though Scripture doesn't have a nice little dissertation laid out for us, Scripture is clear. Life in the womb matters to God. Life doesn't start being valuable or interesting or important only after the transition from inside another body to outside occurs. Life before birth, whether its implications are good or bad, does matter to God. And not only does it matter to God, God is involved in this prebirth life in real and fundamental ways. Although we may not understand it well, embryonic life is still life lived fully in the presence of God.

WHY DIDN'T GOD RESCUE MY PREGNANCY?

So, I had come to an answer to my first question. At least according to the nature of God we see portrayed in Scripture, when asked, "Did God care about unborn life?" I could answer yes. Unborn life is still life lived in the presence of God. This forced me to confront my next question, which was even more personal: If God did care about unborn life, then why didn't God keep my unborn baby alive? Was God powerless to prevent the miscarriage, powerless to rightly form this particular baby? Or did God *will* this pregnancy to end? Did God "do it on purpose," either as part of some larger plan or—God forbid—as some sort of divine punishment?

This, of course, is the classic question. "If God is both good and all-powerful, why is there suffering in the world?" Generation after generation has wrestled with it, coming up with plenty of answers, some more satisfactory than others. I discovered that when it came to pregnancy loss, people were much too prone to simplify their response in a way that trivialized the loss. Most answers fell into one of two categories: (1) "God couldn't do anything" and (2) "Everything is meant to be." Let's look at these separately.

"God Couldn't Do Anything"

One way of resolving the tangle between God's goodness and the existence of suffering is to say that God can't do anything about it. In other words, take God's power out of the equation, remove God's ability to affect human circumstances, and you're left with no contradictions between God's love and human suffering. Of course, you are also left with a rather unimpressive God. A version of this view is *deism*: there is a God, but this God is an impersonal deity who got the world started and then stepped back to let cause and effect, chance and serendipity run their respective collision courses. In the midst of suffering, people may fall back on this position to prevent themselves from blaming God. After all, if God were all-powerful and allowed or—even worse—*caused* this to happen, then God would be the last one to whom that suffering person would want to turn. Mary, who offered her reflections about losing a cherished pregnancy after ten weeks, put it this way:

> I [would] rather not believe in God than [in] a God who does not intervene on our behalf. I see terrible, abusive people hav[ing] children, lots of children, and they neglect and abuse their babies. God either does not care or does not exist. I [would] rather [he] not exist . . . I don't want to have anything to do with him if he will not have anything to do with us . . . I see life as much more chance than I used to.

This is a very common way of coming to terms with deep suffering despite God's existence. It makes sense. Imagine it in human terms. Imagine that I see someone I love, someone for whom I am responsible, in grave danger, and I have the ability to intervene and save her from that danger. If I choose not to intervene, and that person suffers from my inaction, I am responsible for that person's suffering. And it's hard to imagine how I could actually love the one I allowed to suffer. Parents who do that get locked up: parents who are neglectful, who let their toddlers play on the interstate, who say, "Go ahead and touch the hot stove."

The last thing we can accept is that God is this kind of parent. So either we carry deep anger toward a God who seems cruel and callous, or we conclude that since God must be loving, God must not have the power to be involved in our lives directly. We decide, "God couldn't do anything," or "I don't believe that God is directly involved in the world in these days." And our prayers become lifeless and we feel distanced from this God who impassively watches events play out on earth from far, far away.

"Everything Is Meant to Be"

The other way people try to make sense of the coexistence of both suffering and a good God is to say that everything is meant to be and happens for a reason. During the week after that first miscarriage, I got a sympathy call from a well-meaning person. She asked some questions, and upon discovering that I had completed only a year and a half of school and had a year and a half of commuting yet to go, she exclaimed, "Oh, Elise! I had no idea you had another year left! No wonder you had the miscarriage! God knew that having a baby and finishing school would have just about killed you! And his plans are always perfect." In the ache of my loss, everything about this correlation made me furious. And a tiny part of me feared something like it was true. *Oh, fantastic. So God saw that my planner was full, and decided to kill my baby?* As the weeks went by, I realized that this was part of a widely held belief that actually gives many people deep comfort in the face of suffering. It's stated a lot of different ways: "There's a reason for everything." "God has a perfect plan, and this is part of his perfect plan." "God doesn't give you anything you can't handle."

God's will is mysterious, and we cannot always fathom God's ways. That much is true. But to say that absolutely everything that happens in this world is part of God's "perfect plan" is patently untrue. It's not even scriptural. We see over and over again examples of situations that cannot be reconciled with the will of God. Surely it is not meant to be that tiny children are abused or enslaved or made into prostitutes or soldiers against their will. Surely it is not meant to be that whole peoples are driven from their homes and terrorized and slaughtered. Surely it is not meant to be that mothers watch babies starve, that fathers sink under the burden of being unable to support their families. We see a whole host of circumstances in our world that are clearly the result of some sort of brokenness, not God's perfect dream for creation that is set out in Genesis. "No more," promises God, "shall there be in [the new Jerusalem] an infant that lives but a few days, or an old person who does not live out a lifetime" (Isa. 65:20). But it's easy to understand why this would be another common response to suffering. After all, believing that there is divine purpose for a loss like this gives us a reason to endure it and a reason to continue to love God.

THE MYSTERY OF REDEMPTION

After a time, I wondered if there was another path through this wilderness. Neither the witness of Scripture nor the witness of disciples over the ages, some of whom suffered profoundly, allowed me to rest easy with the quick answers. So I decided to approach the problem another way. What if, instead of asking, "Why did God let my baby die?" I asked, "What is God's ultimate will for creation?" The Westminster Shorter Catechism, the English church's doctrinal teaching tool from the 1640s, said it this way: "Man's chief end is to glorify God, and enjoy Him forever." Another way of putting it is this: God, not out of neediness or lack, but out of the overflowing love among the persons of the Trinity, Father, Son, and Holy Spirit, chose freely to create this world, with us in it. It's a bit like choosing to become parents, as a matter of fact. Ideally, not because of any lack or need in the marriage or the self, but because of the way their love for one another overflows into the world around them, two people decide to invite others to share in that love. And the family is opened, by birth or adoption, to needy, underdeveloped creatures who can be blessed and nurtured by the love of the parents, and who can grow to offer love in return. This is a little like what God does in creation. God's will for God's world, God's family, is that they should reflect the glory of the Creator back to God, and enjoy, delight in, that love forever. This is described in Genesis. Adam and Eve walk with God in the cool of the evening, cherished children delighting in their Parent, the breath of the Holy Spirit brushing their naked bodies, warm and safe in the garden among glorious trees and fruits and cared-for animals.

What happens? Perhaps you remember the story: a serpent, a temptation, a fruit consumed, a rule disobeyed. Suddenly fingers are pointing, the peace is broken, and the perfect garden becomes a thing of the past. The implications are complex, but the bottom line is this: God gave humans freedom, to obey or not to obey, to love or not to love. And we chose the path of disobedience, the path of non-trust, of non-love. In that choosing, not only humans, but all of creation somehow got twisted and broken. The lion would now eat the lamb, the wolf would now destroy the kid, if given half a chance. Only through toil and pain would the earth now bring forth good things. Even the act of bringing forth children would now be painful, dangerous, and less certain, less safe. And we no longer know how to walk with God intimately;

we spend our lives feeling alone, or trying to push through murk and muck to see the God we instinctively feel must be there, just beyond our troubled sight. So we hurt one another, and we grasp for more and more, and our world floods, and our earth quakes, and our babies die.

And what happens to God? Where does God go in all this chaos and catastrophe? This is where we return to the loving and perfect plans of God. Our Scriptures tell the story of the lengths to which God will go to bend things back toward wholeness again. First, God created and called a people, a people through whom the entire world would be blessed (Gen. 12:1–4). Centuries elapsed, during which God disciplined and wooed, called and cajoled this people. It became clear that despite moments of hope, moments of promise, God's people proved unable to redeem this world through their obedience, through their striving. Probably God knew they would not—knew that no one could—but was preparing them for the great thing God was about to do. Because into the midst of this precious people, God came in person. Not just in spirit or in voice, as God had done before, but in flesh. Into the midst of a world that was broken and bleeding, God placed God's own self, in the womb of a poor teenaged girl. Borne and born in utter dependence, like any other baby, Jesus grew to young manhood, fully human, fully God-with-us.

And then God "allowed" us to murder God-with-us.

The physical death of Jesus on the cross was painful, horrible, to be sure. But don't miss the other thing that happens here. *God, Godself, is ruptured.* Father, Son, Holy Spirit, that perfect overflowing of love that splashed out into creation, that dance of perfect intimacy—the Son plunges himself into our deepest brokenness and all creation dies a little as death enters into the heart of God. But the deep love-being of God is stronger than death. Instead of being consumed by death, God's love enters, encompasses, and conquers death.

And here is the only answer that takes seriously our deepest pain. Creation was intended to be gloriously good, yet creation has fallen into sickness and suffering. So God has entered into this creation and taken the depths of its sickness, the depths of its suffering, into God's own self. This is not painless. It is costly to God. But our God does not shrink from our suffering. Our God does not retreat to some heavenly sanctuary to watch us, like some impassive giant. Our God does not even settle for imagining, in God's infinite imagination, what our situation must be. Instead, God shows up in person to experience our grief, to lay hands upon our broken bodies, to feel the pain and plight and limits of our existence. But in taking on our sinsickness and suffering, God has done something through the physical world that transcends the physical world. Yes, this act of becoming embodied is an act of eternal significance. God has broken into the trajectory of human history and set it on a different course. Instead of our brokenness leading ultimately to despair and death, our brokenness now leads *through* despair and death into God's redemption of all creation.

Here in the confines of the lives we lead, we don't see the results of this very clearly. We catch only glimpses of it, see only faint glimmers of hope. But because of what God has chosen to do, creation is now headed in a different direction. Now at the end of creation's story is wholeness, healing, God's glorious love once again flowing into creation and freely back again. In the meantime, death is real. Misery is real. Some of us are martyred, some of us are hurt tragically, some of us lose our babies. We walk through floodwaters that are not part of God's intention for God's good creation. But we walk accompanied by the God we killed, the God who took the suffering of the world into God's own heart and God's own incarnate body. And we walk forward trusting in God's ultimate plan for God's broken creation—that God "will wipe every tear from [our] eyes. Death will be no more; mourning and crying and pain will be no more, for the first things have passed away" (Rev. 21:4).

This is not a tidy answer to the question "Why did God let my baby die?" It leaves many questions unanswered and doesn't tie down knowledge of God's will in each particular circumstance. But Christians trust that it is true. We suffer, sometimes profoundly. But we trust that neither suffering nor even death can separate us—or the babies we have loved—from the presence and love of God (Rom. 8:39).

REFLECTION QUESTIONS

1. Did you wonder about God's role during your miscarriage? Why or why not?
2. What do you think God might want to say to you about the loss of your pregnancy?

EXERCISE

Write a letter to God about your miscarriage. Be as blunt as you like. Ask whatever questions you have. Tell God about your experience, how it felt, what you thought. Explain to God what your needs are now. When you are finished, you may share your letter with someone (your partner, your pastor, a trusted Christian friend or spiritual adviser), you may burn or bury your letter, or you may choose to keep it. In any case, God will have received it.

Chapter 6

What about the Baby?

*F*or some people, this section is going to seem like a no-brainer. "Of course God is taking care of the baby," they will say. "Of course the baby's life continues in God." If this is you, you may wish to skip this chapter. But for me, at the time of our first miscarriage, I wasn't so sure. This may sound like a strange thing for a pastor to say. However, here was the issue: Faithful Christians (including many theologians) disagree vehemently about whether or not the pregnancy could even be considered a "person" capable of salvation at a few weeks' gestation. Faithful Christians disagree about the necessity of baptism for salvation. My inquiries into Scripture that I described in the last chapter led me in a particular direction, but they didn't change the fact that many people doubt the personhood of a fetus in the early stages of development.

What made matters worse were the convoluted arguments I was finding on Web sites and in articles that dealt with abortion, both for and against. Pro-choicers were absolutely determined to make the case that early-term abortion dealt with tissue, not a baby. Pro-lifers were absolutely determined to make the case that early-term abortion ended a real life. One pro-life article actually argued that unborn, unbaptized children who die (due to abortion, although the implication for miscarriage is clear) must wind up in purgatory; otherwise, the argument went, if they wound up in heaven, God would be a supporter of abortion.

Both sides appealed to biology to make their case. I read article after article, book after book, of long arguments that characterized fetuses as babies or as nonpeople, as children or as tissue. "When does the soul come to inhabit the body?" asked several pieces of literature. Was it at the moment of conception? Was it at quickening, the moment when the mother first felt the baby move? Was there some special biological stage of development at which everyone could agree, "Ah, now this—*this* is a person"?

This is tough territory. And because it's tough, I think that we Christians have not dealt with it very well. No matter where we have placed ourselves along the broad spectrum of opinions about unborn life, we have allowed a certain cultural way of understanding life to shape our beliefs. *We have based our conversations about pre-born life on biological determinism.* In other words, we've given in to a worldview that says that things are "real" only if we can fit them through a scientific rubric, a series of tests of hypotheses, a set of objectively proven data. Water boils at a certain temperature, the earth is round, germs cause disease . . . and because this is one reliable way of knowing things, we have decided that all truth that is worthwhile has to be discovered in the same way. We expect that life, personhood, will be something we can prove as well.

During the year that I was teaching and learning at Hanover College, I tried an exercise with my introductory theology students that had been developed by one of the other professors in the department. He would start the year by sending his students home with an assignment. "I want you to write a proof for next time," he'd say. "Prove to me the following three things: (1) the existence of the cross outside the Sigma Chi house, (2) that you ate a meal this week, and (3) that your parents love you." Inevitably, the students would come back with sensory proofs for the first two. "I have a photo on my phone—I can show you the cross." "I ate fried chicken, three witnesses saw me eat it, and I can prove it if you want to pump my stomach." But the third was trickier. The conversations I had with my own students went something like this:

A sophomore might begin, "Well, I know my parents love me because they sacrificed a lot to bring me up."

I'd respond, "That's just the biological drive to further the species."

"Huh?" the student would blink.

"That's not love," I'd explain. "Your parents knew that they had to take care of you to enable you to grow up and have kids of your own. It's innate. They couldn't help it."

"Well," the student might counter, "my parents worked hard to save a ton of money so they could send me to school."

"Enlightened altruism," I'd scoff. "They want to be taken care of in their old age, and there's no way you can afford to support them financially if they don't invest in your career preparation now."

The students would start to become uncomfortable at this point. They'd start to toss things out a little frantically, sifting through memories and throwing out whatever they could think of that seemed loving. I would shoot them all down briefly, adding whatever psychological or biological explanations occurred to me. Finally, one young man, a football player, was confused and upset and almost in tears. "I just *know* they love me, OK? It doesn't matter what you say! I know what the *truth* is!"

You see, my students, the same as you and I, have based many of the most important things in their lives on truths that cannot be proved empirically—truths that, in fact, could have many other scientific explanations. Even though we often argue as if we've bought into the modern idea that there's no way of knowing truth except through rational, scientific categories, most of us live differently. We live as if things like love, honor, kindness, and courage are more than biobehavioral instincts meant to further the species. We live as if not everything can be reduced to a set of biological instincts or qualities. We live as if human life has a quality of mystery and beauty and value that goes far beyond scientific determinism.

Those of us who are Christians believe more than even this. We believe in a God who also cannot be proven empirically, but who is nonetheless the ground of all reality, somehow more real than things we can test and measure, just as love is, in a sense, more real than a concrete cross outside a fraternity house. And this is why most of those participating in the abortion debate, Christians especially, have missed the boat. Trying to establish an objectively verifiable definition of "personhood" about which everyone in both sacred and secular circles will agree is misguided, because it assumes that the most important things about us, about living humans, are objectively measurable, provable in a laboratory.

Different folks have tried hard. Some people have tried to say that life is "real life" or fully human when a fetus reaches biological milestones: after the placenta is fully formed, for example, or after the baby has attained a certain level of brain function. There are two problems with this. First, it is often impossible to tell when these milestones have been reached and it is arbitrary *which* milestones should be significant. Second, it is almost always possible to point to humans who lack biological characteristics such as brain function, persons who are close to death or in a coma.

Others have tried to make these arguments in terms of capacity for relationship; in other words, a life is not real until it has the biological capacity to respond to another person, until it can hear and respond to sounds, or respond to pain stimuli. But again, the tests are arbitrary—who, after all, decides which capacities should be the most important, the most constitutive of our personhood?—and we can see plenty of persons who, because of disability or injury, lack those particular capacities for relationship. No matter how hard we try, if we try to develop a concrete understanding of personhood that biology will *prove* for us, we will come up short.

PERSONHOOD AND SALVATION

Theologically, one way of defining personhood is to describe a person as "one who is capable of receiving salvation" or "one who is capable of being in transformative relationship with God." Most of us would probably agree that a blade of grass is not a person in this sense, while our pastor or best friend clearly is. So, we return to the same question from a slightly different perspective: is an unborn baby a person? Unborn life matters to God, as we saw in chapter 5, but is such unborn life capable of receiving God's salvation, even at very early stages? What sort of life, if any, is in store for lost pregnancies?

Historically, Christians haven't had much to say about this. There's a huge, aching void. Since the lives of our lost pregnancies are too important to be left in that vacuum, many of us have filled that empty space with our best, most beautiful visions about life after death. Perhaps you have imagined such visions. Many women hope that their unique little person will get another chance at life, perhaps with another body. Mary shared poignantly:

> [My friend] actually planted the seed of hope, saying, "Maybe the baby wanted a better birthday and will catch the next bus." Wow. . . . That gave me a lot of hope. The baby really isn't gone, it is just waiting for "the next bus." She is Catholic and the "next bus" rings a little of reincarnation, but neither of us got hung up in the dogma. The idea is that there is another chance. If not with me, maybe another nice family.

Another woman said, "I wondered if those babies were just gone, or would they somehow be given new life with someone else? But genetically, this would make no sense." In this vision, we name the infinite uniqueness of each human being, each lost unborn baby. We envision ways that those unique people might continue to grow and develop, even after they have been lost to us.

Some women find great comfort in envisioning their unborn babies as angels. Our knowledge of angels is limited, but we know that they are beings who live in the direct, unmediated presence of God, that they sing God's praises and are safe in God's household forever, resplendent, beautiful, and whole. And so imagining our babies as angels helps us understand those babies as being secure in God's presence, singing God's praises. One woman said, "I later felt that baby angels were needed in heaven."

Others of us try to imagine what it might look like for the life of the unborn baby to continue in heaven, connected to God and to other loved ones. The primary concern for many women is the care of the child whose life was lost, and envisioning their babies in heaven alongside other loved ones who have died reassures them that the babies will be well cared for. Katherine said, "I know my boys are with God. My Mom died shortly after the birth of our only live child, and I know she watches over our two [miscarried] sons."

Personally, in the midst of my feelings of betrayal and anger at God, I did not trust that God would even notice my tiny addition to the ranks of all those who have died. But my beloved great-aunt Mabel died the day before the miscarriage. She had never had children of her own, but she had been a uniquely tender beacon of maternal love, acceptance, peace, and care for more people than I could count, and she was a devout and devoted Swedish Lutheran. I *did* trust *her*. One of the last letters she'd received had been one I'd written, in which I had detailed our joy over the pregnancy, and I knew she would notice our little one, the child-life I agonized would be forgotten or overlooked. I imagined that perhaps her mother-heart would be able to rescue and nurture the baby I had so spectacularly failed to care for. I knew exactly how questionable all this was, but I didn't care. The church, the communion of saints over time, gave me nothing better. And it broke me to pieces to think of the loved child-life I had lost swirling through the sewer forever, or at least until judgment day.

This is where others of us end up, as Serene Jones says in one of the powerful essays in *Hope Deferred*: "I could have promised [my friend] that this hoped-for child was waiting for her in heaven and that, one day, they would dwell together in God's presence. But if I had said this, I would have been lying. I simply didn't believe that all our miscarried hopes were wandering around in heaven waiting for mommy to show up."[1] One woman said, "I sometimes wonder if my little embryo had a soul. I don't think so. It was a tragedy that I think about almost every day, but it never really had a chance to live, therefore I don't think it 'died.' It was a missed opportunity, an unfulfilled dream, maybe not a 'life.' " The silence of the church's tradition leaves a void that we fill in different ways.

After all, in different Christian traditions, salvation is usually connected to baptism or a profession of faith, or both. Neither of these things is possible for a miscarried fetus. There is no opportunity for the church to claim the child and make vows on her behalf; there is no opportunity for the little one to grow into grace and respond to God's love for himself. These are the ways in which the church recognizes persons, those capable of receiving the new life offered in Christ Jesus. With silence resounding from the community of faith, we develop our own ideas and create new communities. This was brought home to me powerfully when I ran across a Web site that offered "Certificates of Graduation to Heaven" for parents to fill out for their miscarried children. We are desperate to know what becomes of the still-beloved little ones we carried, and so we ask an Internet site to certify that they have graduated to heaven.

PERSONHOOD—CONSTITUTED BY RELATIONSHIP WITH GOD

The ground of all our personal visions of what will become of our lost babies is the steadfast love of God. I wonder if we might make that our starting place. Let's leave behind biological determinism; let's leave behind claims that personhood is equivalent to a particular kind of biological development. And let's take a moment to see if the truth contained in Scripture, the truth our visions point us toward and in which our visions are grounded, might give us another way of understanding what salvation might look like for miscarried persons. What if, instead of imagining that personhood is biological, we imagined that personhood could be based on being in relation with God, the God of steadfast love?

This is the point of view offered by the Greek Orthodox theologian John Zizioulas in his classic text *Being as Communion*. In it, he argues that personhood is not primarily a matter of substance (what we're made of, or what we can do) but is understood as a *relational* category of being. The unusual thing about his perspective is that he claims that this being-in-relationship does not "belong to the level of will and action but to that of substance." Being-in-relationship, in other words, does not mean you must be able to have certain kinds of interactions or do certain things. Again, this is a critical point not only for understanding the personhood of the unborn, but equally for understanding the personhood of the mentally disabled, the severely mentally ill, and those who are in nonreactive states (catatonia or coma, for example). Zizioulas claims that personhood is mysterious. And the quality of mystery lies in the fact that love has the ability to give a unique identity, a unique name, to the beloved.[2] Personhood isn't achieved by getting to a certain developmental point, a certain cellular stage of development. Instead, God's love is the ground of all being, and God's love, which is the foundation of all reality, names and gives identity to persons.

Let's say this another way. *There are no intrinsic, developmental, or substantive requirements for a person or thing to be included in the Trinitarian life of God.* A person doesn't have to be a certain size, or be able to count or sing or throw a ball; a person doesn't have to be able to understand love or being, doesn't have to be able to name colors or say where they live. There are no minimum structural or cognitive standards that have to be reached before a person or thing qualifies for the category of personhood. Instead, personhood is constituted (created, even) by love, by relationship. As Zizioulas says, "Love can endow something with uniqueness, with absolute identity and name"[3]—specifically, the love of God in Father, Son, and Holy Spirit, the God who so loved the world that Jesus came to work redemption for the whole creation. The love of God—the love that is in God, that in fact *is* God (1 John 4:8, 16)—provides the foundation for being or personhood as the divine love stretches out to be in relation with other beings.

This is a mystery. It is no scientifically cross-checked statement. It is instead a claim based on the mystery of the Trinity, on the mystery of a relational God who loves and who, in loving, chooses to create, redeem, and sustain creation, regardless of the ability of the different parts of creation to respond in particular ways. Love does not identify a being *capable* of being named; love instead *names*, and in naming, establishes "uniqueness and absolute identity"—personal being, in other words.

Here is the good news. God—the Trinity, Father, Son, and Holy Spirit, joined together in an unending dance of mutual, overflowing love—this God who spoke creation into being is still the ground of its reality, the ground of its being. Stars, soil, sparrows all exist on the breath of God. The things we taste and touch and feel are, in the end, less real than that mighty Love who created them. You and I are only "real" because God scooped and shaped dust and breathed real life into us. And we are only truly "alive" because we were buried in baptism into the grave with Christ and raised to new life on the other side. All our life, such as it is, is based, founded, built on top of the reality of God. We live in every way because God's life undergirds creation. So perhaps it is not so hard to imagine that the tiny, nascent life that was living inside me and the tiny, nascent lives that have lived in so many of you were undergirded by God's reality, made "personal" by the love of the divine Parent.

We can say, then, that an unborn child is a person, not based on biological development, but because we believe that he is loved by the ground of all reality, the Being whose love creates being and grants it to others. Your lost little one was indeed a person, known intimately, loved deeply by our personal God. It doesn't matter how early or how late we die: "If we live, we live to the Lord, and if we die, we die to the Lord; so then, whether we live or whether we die, we are the Lord's. For to this end Christ died and lived again, so that he might be the Lord of both the dead and the living" (Rom. 14:8–9).

At a funeral, a community of believers gathers to remember a life, to mourn its close, and to proclaim their common hope and trust that whatever life looks like on the other side of that deep river separating life from death, it is life lived in the presence of God. This is the posture we take toward those we have lost early to miscarriage. We remember their lives, our hopes and dreams for them, the ways in which their short existence changed us. We mourn their deaths, the deaths that happened in secret places, in the dark of our wombs. And we proclaim our common hope and trust that although we can't wrap our imaginations around the details, the God who holds the span of life and death in God's very hands and even in God's very body, the God who stands beyond the edges of the universe and who dwells within the heart of the atom—this God holds even tiny lost lives in the hollow of the divine hand, calling them by name, knowing them intimately, making them whole and lovely at last.

REFLECTION QUESTIONS

1. Have you imagined what God's ongoing care for a miscarried child might look like? If so, what was your vision like?
2. What hopes do you have for your lost baby, in terms of his or her life in God's keeping? Could you pray, asking God to fulfill these hopes? Why or why not?

EXERCISE

"Love does not identify a being *capable* of being named; love instead *names.*" Have you thought of a name for your lost baby? In the next week, talk with your partner if you like and choose a name for your child, then record that name somewhere. (You could find a smooth stone to write it on, or you could record it in a family Bible or in a special keepsake card.)

Chapter 7

Connected to the Life of God

*O*ne night, a few weeks after our first miscarriage, I sat cross-legged on the shaggy carpeting in my Durham digs, my laptop in front of me, trying to get some writing done. I was spending more time staring into space and starting and abandoning games of FreeCell than I was getting any actual work accomplished. Finally, I brought up a new document and began to write what started as meditations about our loss and ended up looking like a letter to God. Over and over again, I wrote questions about the baby. Where was she? Or *was* she at all? I loved her, yearned over her, was desperate to know what had become of her, was aching to reassure her somehow that she was not alone, was still loved, hadn't been abandoned. But would those reassurances be true?

Many Christians who lose loved ones face similar questions about the connection between the living and those the writer of Hebrews calls the "great cloud of witnesses" (Heb. 12:1). Sometimes we seem to be only a breath away from those who have gone "beyond the veil," and sometimes those we have loved and lost seem to be simply gone. It doesn't seem consistent for Jesus' disciples to believe in ghosts or to hold séances, and yet we want so desperately for those connections, those relationships, to endure.

Fortunately, this is a place where our Christian heritage is *not* silent. We don't have to make up stories to convince ourselves that the babies we have loved and lost are connected still, both to us and to the God who loves both them and us. This does not mean that we'll be haunted by tiny poltergeists or that our lost little ones will become cartoonish angels on our shoulders. It does mean this: those who belong to God are connected eternally to one another through the One who has adopted us as children. You may have heard it said that blood is thicker than water; well, the waters of our baptism are "thicker" than our genetic heritage, and Jesus' blood flows through our veins, connecting us to the Source of all life.

CONNECTED AT THE TABLE

Faithful Christians believe various things about Communion; I am talking out of my own United Methodist heritage. But whether you see the Lord's Supper as an ordinance or a sacrament, whether you receive it twice a year or every week, whether your bread and juice or wine come from prepackaged containers or a common loaf and cup, two connections are represented in that holy act: our connection to the body of Christ and our connection to God's promised new creation.

Connected to the Body of Christ

First is our connection to the body of Christ. "I am the bread of life," Jesus taught. "I am the living bread that came down from heaven. Whoever eats of this bread will live forever; and the bread that I will give for the life of the world is my flesh" (John 6:48, 51). Then at that Last Supper he shared with his disciples, his friends, Jesus held a loaf of bread out to them and said, "This is my body, which is given for you"; he took the cup of wine and said, "This cup that is poured out for you is the new covenant in my blood" (Luke 22:19–20). What does this mean? It means that when we take bread together, when we put the wafer or the torn scrap of loaf on our tongues, we are in some mysterious way sharing in Jesus' own body. When we drink wine together, when we sip the strong port or the sweet grape juice, we are in some mysterious way sharing in Jesus' own blood. Those simple acts of kneeling, receiving, tasting— they splice us into an organism larger than we know. Paul puts it this way:

> The cup of blessing that we bless, is it not a sharing in the blood of Christ? The bread that we break, is it not a sharing in the body of Christ? Because there is one bread, we who are many are one body, for we all partake of the one bread. (1 Cor. 10:16–17)

Did you catch the leap Paul makes? Not only does our sharing of Communion connect us in a fundamental way to Christ, it connects us to Christ's body, to one another. It's as if when we are adopted by God, we're taken up into one vast organism, the body of Christ. We belong to Christ, and we belong to one another—no, more—we *become* part of Christ; we *become* part of one another, deeply, inextricably. Paul also writes:

> For as in one body we have many members, and not all the members have the same function, so we, who are many, are one body in Christ, and individually we are members one of another. (Rom. 12:4–5)

> If one member suffers, all suffer together with it; if one member is hon-
> ored, all rejoice together with it. Now you are the body of Christ and indi-
> vidually members of it. (1 Cor. 12:26–27)

What could be more inextricably connected than the parts of a human body? Strung delicately together on a webbing of nerves and blood vessels and muscle fibers, supported by a strong skeletal structure, and wrapped in a liv-ing casing of skin: when it's healthy, all the parts of the body work in con-cert, elegantly coordinating breaths and thoughts and heartbeats and motions with no conscious effort at all. This, Paul claims, is the strong interconnec-tion of those who belong to Christ. God's children are Christ's very body, the "fullness of him who fills all in all" (Eph. 1:23).

Think, then, what this means for those members of our community who are not yet born. Although we do not see an unborn child with our eyes, touch him with our fingers, he is nestled deep within his mother's own body and nestled deep within, therefore, the body of Christ. As his mother kneels, cups her hands, dips bread into wine, and shares in Christ's body and blood, his nascent body approaches the altar and shares that body and blood as well. Even as his mother is connected in that act to every part of the "one body"—to Christians flung out across time and space, across generations and continents, connected to those who have lived their span on earth and those who are yet to be born—so too is he connected to the communion of saints across the ages. "There is only one body," claims Paul, and the unborn child lives within the very womb of that body—connected firmly to the body of Christ, connected inextricably to the other members of that same body. This is expressed beautifully in a Catholic hymn: "One is the body, one is the bread; One are the living, the unborn, the dead."[1]

Connected to the Coming Kingdom

The second connection that is represented in the Lord's Supper is our con-nection to God's promised coming kingdom, our connection to the good end God has in store for creation. Our Scriptures use feast or banquet imagery over and over again to talk about what it will be like when God makes all things new and right and beautiful at last. The prophet Isaiah, in describing that longed-for moment, says this:

> On this mountain the LORD of hosts will make for all peoples
>   a feast of rich food, a feast of well-aged wines,
>   of rich food filled with marrow, of well-aged wines strained clear.

> And he will destroy on this mountain
>> the shroud that is cast over all peoples,
>> the sheet that is spread over all nations;
>> he will swallow up death forever.

(Isa. 25:6–8)

"Then," says Jesus in Luke, "people will come from east and west, from north and south, and will eat in the kingdom of God" (Luke 13:29). Jesus tells a parable comparing the kingdom of heaven to the wedding banquet a king throws for his son. And in Revelation, John records that toward the end of his vision "the angel said to me, 'Write this: Blessed are those who are invited to the marriage supper of the Lamb'" (Rev. 19:9).

This is what we are proclaiming, what we are in some way anticipating, when we share the smaller Communion feast. As we are joined to Christ, we are joined to his resurrection as well as his life and death. As we are connected to the life of the one who was fully human, fully divine, we flash forward to the "marriage supper," the wedding banquet of a Prince. And we, the church, are the bride.

Time gets gathered up in Communion. It's as if a holy needle passes through us at the Table, gathering us onto a long thread, the thread of the story of salvation. We are collected on that thread along with God's people across time, connected from the knot on the end that holds the beginnings of our common story all the way to the future point at which we'll gather around a table the likes of which we have never seen before. Just as pleats are gathered on a waistband, we will be gathered together, connected full circle. For now, we get hints, glimpses of the span of that thread, as we gather to eat, drink, and "proclaim the Lord's death until he comes again." The United Methodist service calls Communion a "foretaste of the heavenly banquet." At the Table, we are connected to God's ultimate desire for all creation, connected to the day when Christ will be all in all.

What does this mean for the unborn baby? I think one of Paul's analogies can help us here. In talking to the Corinthians about the difference between the bodies they have now and the bodies they will have in the resurrection, he says:

> But someone will ask, "How are the dead raised? With what kind of body do they come?" Fool! What you sow does not come to life unless it dies. And as for what you sow, you do not sow the body that is to be, but a bare seed, perhaps of wheat or of some other grain. But God gives it a body as he has chosen, and to each kind of seed its own body. . . . So it is with the resurrection of the dead. What is sown is perishable, what is raised is imperishable. It is sown in dishonor, it is raised in glory. It is sown in

weakness, it is raised in power. It is sown a physical body, it is raised a spiritual body." (1 Cor. 15:35–38, 42–44)

Paul is using an incredibly important metaphor here. People are asking him what the resurrection body is like; in other words, they are asking him about the *connection* between their current body and the body they will have on the other side of death. You can imagine what someone has said: "You see me now; I am dark-haired, tall, heavily built, and all these things are true about me and yet they are somehow not *all* that is true about me. How will I know who I am after I have died and receive a new body? What will I be—*who* will I be—after the resurrection from the dead?" And Paul's response is to make a comparison. "It's like this," he says. "Your body is like a seed. What happens when a seed is planted? The seed itself dies. And a plant grows that looks nothing at all like the seed, but everything that plant is or becomes was contained within that seed from the beginning. So we don't know what your resurrection body will be like; chances are, it will be as different from your current body as a seed is from a plant. But just as that unique, particular plant grows only from that unique, particular seed, you will be *you* in the resurrection. The potential for everything you will be—glorious, imperishable, spiritual—is held inside you now."

Just as a seed is firmly connected to the plant it will become, so too our bodies are firmly connected to our resurrection selves, the other side of death. So too our unborn babies, those seeds of promise, are connected to their own resurrection selves, their own ends, on the other side of death. At the Table, just as we receive a foretaste of the marriage feast of the Lamb, just as we are connected to the end of God's story, to the time when all will be made new and beautiful, when everything will finally live into its promise, live into God's dream for creation, so too at the Table our unborn children are connected to God's dream for their lives.

Practically Speaking

Mystical connections are all very well, you may be saying, but what difference does it make that our lost babies were and are connected to us and to the rest of the body of Christ, that they were and are connected to God's dream for creation? Practically, I think this means two things. First, it means that we can trust that members of God's family who die before they are born are still held within the connection of God's beloved community. Second, it means that we are not only allowed but also called to pray for these members of God's community. Martin Luther, whose own wife suffered at least one miscarriage, wrote a treatise on the topic:

> It often happens that devout parents, particularly the wives, have sought consolation from us because they have suffered such agony and heartbreak in child-bearing when, despite their best intentions and against their will, there was a premature birth or miscarriage and their child died at birth or was born dead. . . . Because the mother is a believing Christian it is to be hoped that her heartfelt cry and deep longing to bring her child to be baptized will be accepted by God as an effective prayer. . . . Who can doubt that those Israelite children who died before they could be circumcised on the eighth day were yet saved by the prayers of their parents in view of the promise that God willed to be their God? God (they say) has not limited his power to the sacraments, but has made a covenant with us through his word. . . . Therefore one must leave such situations to God and take comfort in the thought that he surely has heard our unspoken yearning and done all things better than we could have asked. In summary, see to it that above all else you are a true Christian and that you teach a heartfelt yearning and praying to God in true faith, be it in this or any other trouble. Then do not be dismayed or grieved about your child or yourself, and know that your prayer is pleasing to God and that God will do everything much better than you can comprehend or desire. "Call upon me," he says in Psalm 50 [:15], "in the day of trouble; I will deliver you, and you shall glorify me." . . . God intends that his promise and our prayer or yearning which is grounded in that promise should not be disdained or rejected, but be highly valued and esteemed.[2]

We are not only permitted to pray for these unborn members of the community, we *ought* to pray for them.[3]

CONNECTED TO THE LIFE OF GOD

There is one more crucial connection. Christians understand God as existing eternally in three persons: Father, Son, and Holy Spirit. This is not the place for an in-depth exploration of the Trinity, but understanding God as existing forever in community—three persons bound in love, distinct yet unified—can help us understand the depths of the love that God has lavished on us. What happens if we, God's children, are inextricably connected to the Son, if we become his body, he our head? We have become bound to the Son, who is bound to the Father and the Spirit; in other words, we have been incorporated, taken up, into the whole life of God. This is what redemption looks like. We are brought back into intimate belonging with the triune God.

Some women, although they want to feel close to God, although they want to believe that God cares, feel as if God is incredibly removed from the pain of losing a pregnancy. They feel as if their loss was minute, so small that the God of the universe, the God who is watching over the whole world, could not possibly be affected by it in the same way they are. There is no way, they may think, that God knows what they're going through. Pastors often invoke Jesus as the holy sympathizer, saying, "He's been through everything you've been through. He knows how it feels." But for women in particular, this comparison may feel hollow. As much as Jesus, God-with-us, did share the human condition, shared temptation and hunger and exhaustion, he did not, in all likelihood, share the conditions of female embodiment. It is more than probable that Jesus did not suffer menstrual cramps, experience labor, or nurse a baby. And so it can be tough to imagine that God knows, really *knows*, what it feels like to have a uterus that is pouring blood, what it feels like to lose a pregnancy.

Some people have tried to make the experiential leap for parents who have lost a living child, saying that God knows what it is like to lose a son. This is a helpful image for many parents who have lost children, but it can make people who have had miscarriages feel even more isolated. Of course God takes seriously the loss of a living child; who doesn't? But there are so many who don't understand the loss of an unborn child, who don't think that miscarriage is a legitimate grief. How can we be sure that God understands *this* pain? How can we know that God cares about *this* loss?

As we mentioned before, some women find out that the baby has died before they are aware of the miscarriage. They go in to have an ultrasound or a sonogram and there is no heartbeat. The baby on the screen is not moving. From that moment until the mother's body begins spontaneously miscarrying or until the D&C, the mother is holding death within her body. Tammy describes her experience this way:

> My husband was already in Iraq (military) by the time I had found out I was pregnant. I had the ultrasound at six weeks and saw and heard the baby's heartbeat and was told all looked normal. . . . Three weeks later while visiting family in Tennessee, I began to bleed and was immediately panicked. . . . The ER doctors in Tennessee decided that my baby had died just a day after the ultrasound. I had carried my baby dead in my womb for three weeks. . . . I felt that my womb had become a tomb . . . and still feel that way today.

Heather shared:

> With my first pregnancy (and loss), I had been dealing with infertility for nine years and became pregnant. We saw a heartbeat on two different ultrasounds, but when we went back for our eleven-week ultrasound, the baby had died. I was devastated. I didn't know that a baby's heart could stop beating. We scheduled a D&C for the next morning. . . . The whole evening before the D&C, I wept constantly. I went back and forth between being horrified that there was a dead baby inside me and wanting to stay pregnant.

An ongoing life holding death inside. A mother knowing that her child is "buried" in her very womb, the place that should be, of all places, a place of life. Whether or not a woman has this particular experience of knowing her unborn child is dead while she continues to be pregnant, many women still experience themselves as holding death inside. Their own life continues, although its boundaries seem to be shattered, its edges blurred unrecognizably, by the death that has happened within their very core. How do we know that God understands this unique kind of loss? How can we be sure that God holds us with sympathy as well as compassion? One of the most powerful images I have encountered in response to this question was offered by theologian Serene Jones, who explored the image of the Trinity to help us imagine how miscarriage might give us a glimpse of what happens in the life of God when Jesus goes to the cross.[4] Perhaps, she suggests, miscarriage is in some way an icon of the crucifixion, an image that illuminates what happened in God's life, in the life of the Trinity, as Jesus died.

Christians have searched for images to reflect the mystery of the Trinity since the beginning. You may have heard people suggest that the three-in-one God is a little like an egg (shell, yolk, and white) or water (ice, liquid, and steam) or a tree (roots, trunk, and leaves). None of these images really work, as they imply either that the persons of the Trinity are three separate gods who just happen to be joined up or that God is "Eternal Plastic-Man" (as a seminary professor of mine memorably put it), showing Godself sequentially in three different forms. No, the mystery of the triune God over which hundreds of pages of ink was spilled in the earliest days of the church is more mysterious than any of these images, although the images do help us conceptualize how one thing might be three and yet one. What happens to the God-life in the crucifixion remains mysterious as well.

Think of it this way, Jones suggests: A Mother. A Child. A Love, a Connection that is somehow not either the Mother or the Child nor separate from either of them. A pregnant woman—another image, another icon of the Trinity. Incomplete, like the other images but it helps us imagine how one thing might be three and yet one.

And imagine now: the Child dies. The Mother miscarries. The Love connecting them is severed, yet still existing, all three ripped apart and yet desperate to belong together again. The dance is interrupted; the blessed, blissful union torn; the Life ended and yet ongoing. An image, an icon of what the crucifixion may have been like for the God-life. Incomplete, like the other images, but it helps us imagine in a new way how death might unforgettably alter, wound, the triune life. As the earth quakes and the temple curtain rips, the Godhead feels the Beloved bleed away. Father and Son are separate now. Death has entered the heart of God, the womb of God.

Here is the source of Christian hope. We can never be so separated—by conflict, by hurt, even by death—that God cannot bring us back together. For Jesus has left the life of God to travel as far as the bounds of death itself, has encompassed death, and has brought it back within God's reach. And so both on this side of death and beyond it, we are held by the One who underwent death so we would not face it alone. Even those small miscarried lives, separated from us by a blank of memory, of unlived life, of death, cannot go so far that they are beyond the reach of God, beyond God's power to bring them back into the beloved community. This is the power of the resurrection: Jesus has been raised, death has been conquered, and we have nothing more to fear. Our babies, too, rest secure in the arms of this God, the God apart from whose knowledge not even a sparrow falls.

REFLECTION QUESTIONS

1. Have you prayed for your unborn baby since your miscarriage? Why or why not?
2. Does it make any difference to you to imagine that God might understand your grief and your pain in an intimate and personal way? If so, what difference? If not, why not?

EXERCISE

Write a prayer for your baby. Include in it your ultimate hopes for the baby's future, especially those you might have reflected on at the end of chapter 6. Express, as Luther says, your heartfelt yearning on your baby's behalf.

Chapter 8

Relating to God after a Miscarriage

We hope that God cares for unborn members of the community, that unborn babies are treated by God as beloved persons, that God is able to weave a thread of grace in the midst of the tragedy of miscarriage. Even so, the reality of our experience is that after a miscarriage, our relationship with God will be affected, for better or for worse. Losses transform us, and as we are transformed our relationships with others shift in response—not least, our relationship with God. Every person will notice different transitions in that relationship, depending on your prior relationship, your personal history, your experience of miscarriage, and your understanding of God's character and activity in the world. Many women experience powerful negative emotions directed toward God, while others find that their trust and faith are paradoxically strengthened. *There is no "right way" to feel toward God after your loss.* Do not feel as if to be a good Christian you have to accept your loss, to immediately find meaning in it, or to pretend to be happy with God when you are not. One of the precious, life-giving things about our Scripture is that it contains searing prayers of anger, betrayal, bewilderment, longing, and doubt. These are all legitimate ways for the people of God to feel toward their God. God is big enough to receive your doubt, your anger, your bitterness. God does not need to be protected from real grief and emotions.

We will walk together through common ways people feel toward God after miscarriage. Perhaps you will see a reflection of your own feelings in the stories below. At the end of each section is a psalm that expresses similar feelings. Authentic relationship means bringing to the other your true self, no matter what state you are in. Whether you curse God or cry out to God, God wants to be in authentic relationship with you.

ANGER

This is a scary emotion for many women to feel and recognize. Many of us have been taught that nice girls don't get angry, and it can be unsettling to sense rage toward God (of all targets!) rising up in you, but anger is one of the most common emotions people feel toward God after miscarriage. Katherine said, "I was very angry at God after both losses . . . perhaps more so with our second loss. I have been a good person my whole life, and I didn't understand why I would be chosen to face this kind of horrible loss. I was hurt and angry that my chances to finally have a child were taken from me, in death."

"I was angry," Debbie said. " 'Why me?' went through my mind a lot. The only thing I wanted to be growing up was [to be] a wife and mother. I felt like a total failure on the mother end . . . which in the end had an effect on the wife part." Mary confessed, "I'm still angry, sometimes. When I allow myself to be angry, I think, 'I believe in God, I just don't think he believes in us.' He is unfair, unjust, and unreasonable." She continued, "We [God and I] are no longer on speaking terms."

Are you angry? Angry at God, the God who is supposed to create, nourish, and sustain life? Are you resentful that there was no miracle for you, that God didn't intervene at zero hour? Perhaps Psalm 13 can give you some words to pray. (You may also want to look at Pss. 88 or 137.)

Psalm 13

How long, O LORD? Will you forget me forever?
    How long will you hide your face from me?
How long must I bear pain in my soul,
    and have sorrow in my heart all day long?
How long shall my enemy be exalted over me?

Consider me and answer me, O LORD my God!
    Give light to my eyes, or I will sleep the sleep of death,
and my enemy will say, "I have prevailed";
    my foes will rejoice because I am shaken.

But I trusted in your steadfast love;
    my heart shall rejoice in your salvation.
I will sing to the LORD,
    because he has dealt bountifully with me.

DISTRUST

This was one of my own primary reactions. I still thought that God probably existed (although there were nights when I had my doubts), but I was not certain anymore that I could trust this God. If God did not protect my baby, then it was clear that our priorities were in different places. Perhaps the God I thought I had known all these years was a projection of my own desires, and the God who really existed was distant, cold, unknowable. Or worse, perhaps God was vindictive and punishing me for something. I could not trust or love this kind of God. I slunk around in my prayers for weeks, quickly shoving nasty thoughts about this God down to some nether region, wondering if God was frigidly taking note of my anger and distrust, waiting to pounce again.

"At times," said Debbie, "I felt like [the miscarriage] was some kind of punishment. What for, I was not sure."

Are you having trouble trusting God? Does it seem like it's been a lifetime since your faith was characterized by confidence and assurance? Do you wonder if God cares, if God was punishing you for some unknown misstep? The psalmist who wrote Psalm 42 seems to have felt much like this.

Psalm 42:1–4, 9–11

As a deer longs for flowing streams,
    so my soul longs for you, O God.
My soul thirsts for God,
    for the living God.
When shall I come and behold
    the face of God?
My tears have been my food
    day and night,
While people say to me continually,
    "Where is your God?"

These things I remember,
    as I pour out my soul:
how I went with the throng,
    and led them in procession to the house of God,
with glad shouts and songs of thanksgiving,
    a multitude keeping festival.

. . . .

I say to God, my rock,
   "Why have you forgotten me?
Why must I walk around mournfully
   because the enemy oppresses me?"
As with a deadly wound in my body,
   my adversaries taunt me,
while they say to me continually,
   "Where is your God?"

Why are you cast down, O my soul,
   and why are you disquieted within me?
Hope in God; for I shall again praise him,
   my help and my God.

DISTANCE

For some people, distance characterizes their relationship with God. For some, God feels absent, distant, unreachable. Other women feel as though they need to keep God at arm's length. Megan, a pastor married to a pastor, who lost two pregnancies toward the end of the first trimesters, expressed it this way:

> I remember sitting down to eat a meal with Brad, and we always take turns blessing the food. It was my turn and I could not say a word. I started crying, could not stop, and consequently Brad prayed for me. I was shocked that I couldn't even say a simple blessing for my dinner, that even a short, routine prayer was more communication than I wanted with God. It's not good when a pastor can't pray . . . but it became one of those things I asked people to do for me.
>
> . . . You pray so hard for things to turn out right, a continual prayer. And then this happens, and it is like a slap in the face. And I know this is going to sound silly, but through my silence it was like I was punishing God . . . giving God the silent treatment.

Do you feel far away from God? Or do you feel like you need to push God away from you? You may be experiencing a season of waiting, either waiting for God or waiting to allow God near again. This time of waiting on the fringes of God's presence is described by the psalmist.

Psalm 130:1–6

Out of the depths I cry to you, O LORD.
   Lord, hear my voice!

Let your ears be attentive
    to the voice of my supplications!

If you, O LORD, should mark iniquities,
    Lord, who could stand?
But there is forgiveness with you,
    so that you may be revered.
I wait for the LORD, my soul waits,
    and in his word I hope;
my soul waits for the Lord
    more than those who watch for the morning,
    more than those who watch for the morning.

INCREASED TRUST

Some women who continue to feel very close to God throughout their losses discover an increased sense of trust in God. They experience God's steadfast care through their pain and find themselves more certain of God's good intentions toward them and their lost babies. "I didn't question why he did this to me," said Tammy. "I believe he knew in advance that one day he would let me go through the grief and pain and it is for a reason. I don't know if I will ever know the reason(s) but I trust in him for my eternal life and I sure trust that he has done right." For some people this sense of trust, this belief that God is worthy of full confidence even when suffering makes it hard to see, may come early, but for many more it may come only after months or even years have passed. In Psalm 103, the psalmist seems to have known intimately both suffering and the comfort of clinging to God through the valleys.

Psalm 103:1–5, 8–18, 22

Bless the LORD, O my soul,
    and all that is within me,
    bless his holy name.
Bless the LORD, O my soul,
    and do not forget all his benefits—
who forgives all your iniquity,
    who heals all your diseases,
who redeems your life from the Pit,
    who crowns you with steadfast love and mercy,
who satisfies you with good as long as you live,
    so that your youth is renewed like the eagle's.

. . . .

The LORD is merciful and gracious,
   slow to anger and abounding in steadfast love.
He will not always accuse,
   nor will he keep his anger forever.
He does not deal with us according to our sins,
   nor repay us according to our iniquities.
For as the heavens are high above the earth,
   so great is his steadfast love toward those who fear him;
as far as the east is from the west,
   so far he removes our transgressions from us.
As a father has compassion for his children,
   so the LORD has compassion for those who fear him.
For he knows how we were made;
   he remembers that we are dust.

As for mortals, their days are like grass;
   they flourish like a flower of the field;
for the wind passes over it, and it is gone,
   and its place knows it no more.
But the steadfast love of the LORD is from everlasting to everlasting
   on those who fear him,
   and his righteousness to children's children,
to those who keep his covenant
   and remember to do his commandments.
. . . .
Bless the LORD, all his works,
   in all places of his dominion.
Bless the LORD, O my soul.

DEEPER INTIMACY

There are times when deep tragedy or grief knit people much closer together. Some women find this to be the case with their relationship with God after their own loss. Tammy said, almost wonderingly, "My relationship with God grew . . . I felt him more during those days than I ever had before . . . I felt so close with him." Another woman agreed. "I felt closer to God because I leaned on him more than ever." Has this been your experience? Have you been surprised to find that God has seemed nearer to you than ever before, nearer perhaps than in the days of ease and sunshine? The writer of Psalm 116 exhibits this paradoxical combination of the experience of great suffering and the experience of God's sustaining intimacy in the darkest of circumstances.

Psalm 116:1–5, 7–8, 12–15

I love the LORD, because he has heard
   my voice and my supplications.
Because he has inclined his ear to me,
   therefore I will call on him as long as I live.
The snares of death encompassed me;
   the pangs of Sheol laid hold on me;
   I suffered distress and anguish.
Then I called on the name of the LORD:
   "O LORD, I pray, save my life!"

Gracious is the LORD, and righteous;
   our God is merciful.
. . . .
Return, O my soul, to your rest,
   for the LORD has dealt bountifully with you.

For you have delivered my soul from death,
   my eyes from tears,
   my feet from stumbling.
. . . .
What shall I return to the LORD
   for all his bounty to me?
I will lift up the cup of salvation
   and call on the name of the LORD.
I will pay my vows to the LORD
   in the presence of all his people.
Precious in the sight of the LORD
   is the death of his faithful ones.

COMBINATION OF FEELINGS

Many women will experience some combination of feelings toward God: negative and positive, anger and love, doubt and trust. LeAnn expressed this well:

My relationship with God was strengthened after the first miscarriage, but was definitely strained after the second loss. I was very angry with God. I did not understand why he would give us this child and then take it away. I wish that I had been stronger in my faith during that time, but there were times that I could not talk to him. I found some prayers on the Internet that I would read aloud. I continued to go to church and surround myself with the same Christian friends and family. Sometimes I would hear words in contemporary Christian songs on the radio that would be exactly what I was feeling. Those types of experiences were my prayers during a time when I found it hard to pray. My comfort came in knowing that God loved my child (even more than [I]) and created him/her for some reason.

Heather agreed:

I didn't understand how God could let me get pregnant after all that time only to lose the baby, and then I couldn't understand why it kept happening over and over again. I went through a time when I was mad at him. At the same time, I felt very close to him, like he was carrying me through it. I found comfort in leading worship and in spending time with him . . . I believe [my relationship with God] grew stronger [after the miscarriage].

In Psalm 77, the psalmist displays some of this ambiguity in his own emotions. He is raw, open with God about his state. "So troubled that [he] cannot speak," he nevertheless pours out his sense of longing, his grievous pain. In the night, as his eyes burn and sleep eludes him, he wonders aloud where God is, why God seems absent. Then he decides to remember what he knows of God. He rehearses the things God has done in the past, the ways God's steadfast love and delivering hand have been on display to God's people. Even in the midst of his pain and doubt, he calls to mind reasons to trust God, to keep reaching out his hands, to believe that one day he again will be able to sense the presence of the Most High.

Psalm 77

I cry aloud to God,
    aloud to God, that he may hear me.
In the day of my trouble I seek the Lord;
    in the night my hand is stretched out without wearying;
    my soul refuses to be comforted.
I think of God, and I moan;
    I meditate, and my spirit faints.   *Selah.*

You keep my eyelids from closing;
    I am so troubled that I cannot speak.
I consider the days of old,
    and remember the years of long ago.
I commune with my heart in the night;
    I meditate and search my spirit:
"Will the Lord spurn forever,
    and never again be favorable?

Has his steadfast love ceased forever?
    Are his promises at an end for all time?
Has God forgotten to be gracious?
    Has he in anger shut up his compassion?"   *Selah.*
And I say, "It is my grief
    that the right hand of the Most High has changed."

I will call to mind the deeds of the Lord;
    I will remember your wonders of old.
I will meditate on all your work,
    and muse on your mighty deeds.
Your way, O God, is holy.
    What god is so great as our God?
You are the God who works wonders;
    you have displayed your might among the peoples.
With your strong arm you redeemed your people,
    the descendants of Jacob and Joseph.   *Selah.*

When the waters saw you, O God,
    when the waters saw you, they were afraid;
    the very deep trembled.
The clouds poured out water;
    the skies thundered;
    your arrows flashed on every side.
The crash of your thunder was in the whirlwind;
    your lightnings lit up the world;
    the earth trembled and shook.
Your way was through the sea,
    your path, through the mighty waters;
    yet your footprints were unseen.
You led your people like a flock
    by the hand of Moses and Aaron.

The women who submitted interviews had a range of emotional responses and ways of being in relationship with God after their losses. You will have your own response. It will be unique because of your personal history with God, your character and personality, your emotional makeup, and your life story. God knows all these things about you, and God will not expect you to react in any sort of prescribed way. God wants to be with you in the midst of whatever you experience. If you are angry, God wants you to express your anger. If you don't trust God or if you're not even sure that God exists anymore, shout that in God's direction. If you can lean on God more than ever before, lean with full assurance. Whatever state you find yourself in is right. God stands ready to receive you.

THE ROLE OF COMMUNITY

What if you simply don't want to have anything to do with God? What if, as Mary said, you don't feel as if you can be on speaking terms with God? What if, like LeAnn, you are unable to pray? What if, like Megan, even a mealtime blessing feels like more contact than you want with God?

I believe that these are the moments when we need other people who can pray on our behalf. The church, or the community across time and space of those who have given their lives to God, is described in Scripture as a body, as we spoke of in the last chapter, one organic, interdependent whole. If this is true, then you are not abandoned in your inability to relate to God. The part of the body you represent is incapacitated for a time, it is true. But what happens in a human body when one part is injured, unable to fulfill its special role?

I have broken a bone in each foot over the past decade. Both times I wore a cast up to my ankle and had to be on crutches for several weeks. Both times my foot could not do what it was created to do, could not bear the weight of my body flexibly and strongly. For a time it had to hide in the heavy shell of the cast that protected the broken place, giving it a chance to swell and hurt and shift and finally begin the process of healing. Both times, I was amazed by how quickly the rest of my body took over to keep my whole self functioning. My triceps and shoulders went from inconsequential to aching to firm and strong in a matter of days. My sense of balance reconstituted itself with a different allocation of weight. The calf on the uninjured leg popped out with new muscle. And although I was nowhere near as good at getting around on crutches as I was with both feet, I could hop up and down steps and swing myself down the street at a pretty good clip. The rest of my body stepped up to cover my foot's work as it began to heal.

Something a lot like this happens in the body of Christ. Your role is a special and unique one, but just as the body parts have many unique roles that make up one holistic mission, your role within the body of Christ supports the mission of the whole. When you are "broken," often you can no longer fulfill your role or have to fill it partially. You cannot pray. You cannot believe. You cannot minister. And the body (or in this case, the church), perhaps clumsily but always lovingly, accommodates and performs your role for you until you are able to do it again. There is a lovely line in the Hispanic Creed written by United Methodist theologian Justo González that goes like this: "And because we believe, we commit ourselves: To believe for those who do not believe, To love for those who do not love, To dream for those who do not dream, Until the day when hope becomes reality."[1] Following your loss, you may not be able to believe, to love, to dream. You may find that your capacity for all those things is diminished, if not downright destroyed for a time. But remember that in your broken time, there are those who are believing for you, praying for you, loving for you, dreaming for you. The body of Christ surrounds you and does what you are unable to do, until the day when you are able again.

Of course, it is best if this truth is lived out in concrete ways. It is best if you are surrounded by a vibrant, loving, believing faith community, lovers of God who have the gift of comfort and who know how to surround others with love during times of pain. Some of you may have had that gift. Others may have felt very alone, isolated from the community of Christ as well as from other communities. But the truth about being knit into God's body on earth is that even when it is invisible to you, you have been incorporated into the Christ-body. And although they do not know the particulars, nuns in Latin America, new believers in China, Episcopal children in Nebraska, college students at Duke Chapel, are believing for you, praying for you, loving for you during your time of doubt and distance.

REFLECTION QUESTIONS

1. In what ways has your relationship with God changed since your miscarriage?
2. Does it make any difference to feel that you are being prayed for, either by those who know you personally or by those who do not know you at all? Why or why not?

EXERCISE

The hymn that appears below was written by Dietrich Bonhoeffer while he was a prisoner in Nazi Germany. Often those who have experienced suffering can help us find ways to communicate with God when we too are suffering. Read the hymn text below as a prayer. Does it say what you want to say to God? If not, try to write your own prayer to God. Don't worry if words won't come or if the words that come aren't "religious" or seem angry.

By gracious powers so wonderfully sheltered,
and confidently waiting come what may,
we know that God is with us night and morning,
and never fails to greet us each new day.

Yet is this heart by its old foe tormented,
still evil days bring burdens hard to bear;
Oh, give our frightened souls the sure salvation
for which, O Lord, You taught us to prepare.

And when this cup You give is filled to brimming
with bitter suffering, hard to understand,
we take it thankfully and without trembling,
out of so good and so beloved a hand.

Yet when again in this same world You give us
the joy we had, the brightness of Your sun,
we shall remember all the days we lived through,
and our whole life shall then be Yours alone.[2]

PART 3   The Journey Forward

Chapter 9

Who Else Is Hurting?

In the vortex of an intense loss, it is very difficult to be aware of and present to the emotional needs of other people. In the throes of grief, many people have said that we almost *become* the pain, as if there is no way for us to be aware of a self apart from the intensity of the grief. For this reason, it is difficult to nurture relationships while we are hurting.

Miscarriage is an especially complicated loss to deal with in the network of our relationships as well. The woman is the only one who has *directly* experienced the loss, the only one whose body has been affected by the life of the baby, the only one who has direct memories of the changes the life of the baby made within her. For this reason, the pregnancy may not have seemed as real to the other parent or to the grandparents or to the members of the woman's Bible class, and so the grief may be experienced differently.

Furthermore, any sudden or difficult loss exposes the existing weak places in relationships. It's a lot like the stress of holidays, when families under the pressure of the intense emotion and togetherness often associated with big gatherings find otherwise hidden ruptures and conflicts emerging. A conversation about who is going to carve the turkey this year leads into a shouting match about the division of Grandma's estate. An innocent remark about a new roof turns into a standoff about a family member's money management.

On the other hand, times of shared pain and grief can also knit people together more closely than years of peaceful coexistence could ever do. Whether our relationships are further broken and ruptured by stress and grief or strengthened as the grief is survived together is at least partially related to the health of the relationship before the crisis occurred. If you and your partner have built a foundation of intimacy and trust, and if you had a lifetime of intimate, trusting relationships that formed you even before you were married, it is much more likely that weathering storms together will continue to deepen that intimacy and trust, even as it stresses the relationship. Katherine said that her miscarriage "brought my husband and [me] closer together," and another woman agreed, saying, "My husband and I became closer because we felt each other's pain." If, on the other hand, you are carrying around the weight of betrayal and abuse, or if your relationship is already fractured and unstable, the stress of losing a pregnancy can shake a marriage into pieces.

Whichever situation you find yourself in, it can help to have some idea of what your partner or your parents or your other children might be going through. In the next sections, we will look at each of these relationships.

PARTNER/SPOUSE

The men I talked to had remarkably similar reactions to the pregnancy losses they and their wives had experienced. Almost all of them mentioned feeling an enormous responsibility to manage and control their own emotions so that they could be strong to support their wives. Sometimes this meant that they appeared stony or stoic, even uncaring. Most men were assailed by feelings of utter helplessness, especially during the parts of the miscarriage that caused their wives physical pain. Many talked about a confusing sense of guilt that perhaps their wives cared more about the loss than they did. And many men were so incredibly relieved that the mother was all right that they didn't have much emotion to spare for the loss of the pregnancy.

The other particularly difficult aspect of the father's grief is that no one may expect him to suffer from this loss. A 1998 study said that "men are at risk of developing a chronic grief response [after a miscarriage] because they are less likely to receive support and understanding."[1] Men may feel extremely isolated and lonely in their grief. The woman who has experienced the miscarriage tends to be preoccupied as she works through a complicated loss, and although she may not have all the support she needs, she is likely to have some sort of acknowledgment and support from friends and other family members. Often, the men are sort of hung out to dry. They desperately want to help their grieving wives but are often afraid that whatever they do will make things worse.

Most men do feel that their own grief is less intense and lasts for a shorter time than that of their partner. However, men who have seen an ultrasound tend to have a much more intense grief response than those who have not.[2] For them, the pregnancy becomes "real" when they see the ultrasound image of their daughter or son.

You can see why relationships are stressed by miscarriage. One person has experienced the lost life in a direct, intense way, and the other has not. One person has been experiencing morning sickness, strange changes in appetite and smells, sore breasts; the other has heard about these things secondhand, has perhaps brewed ginger tea or gotten up early with the older children, but has not experienced any direct physical changes. One person has had pregnancy hormones coursing through her body, heightening emotions, affecting her moods, her dreams, her feelings; the other has experienced none of these effects of the pregnancy firsthand. And so it does often happen that the woman in whose body the death takes place grieves in a more immediate and intimate way than her partner. However, the grief men *do* feel, whether it is as intense or not, is often overlooked by medical professionals, clergy, and family members.

Moreover, the mother may, in her own grief, resent greatly that her partner does not seem to be taking it as hard as she is. The control he exerts over his own emotions so that he can be present and supportive to her may seem like coldness or indifference. His attempts to care for her by distracting her or focusing on providing for her at work may seem to her like distance from the loss. The very gifts with which he is attempting to comfort his wife may strike her as signs of his lack of feeling. And so without good communication (and sometimes despite it), marriages can suffer greatly. LeAnn, whose marriage was strong both before and after the loss, described her experience this way:

> My grief was very different from my husband's grief. He did not shed tears for weeks or months as I did. He seemed to be more accepting of this being part of God's will than I was. Sometimes I was very angry with him because he did not appear to hurt as much as I did. After our son was born, my husband spoke in church about the baby we lost. I was stunned to know that he even still thought about that baby, and it was a moment that I will always remember.

Christine said, "My husband and I both grieved, but separately, each quietly blaming ourselves." Another woman shared:

> After two miscarriages, my spouse seemed uninterested in trying to have a baby. When I became pregnant a third time, my spouse was uninvolved with the pregnancy. He explained that he had become emotionally tied with the two lost babies, and he could not handle that again. That surprised me since he did not show any emotion when I miscarried. I wondered how he thought I felt.

Mary said, "After a while, a few months maybe, my husband declared that we just couldn't talk about it anymore. There was nothing he could do about it and he just couldn't bear bringing it up again."

Just as every woman's grief is different, however, every man's grief is different as well. You may find that your partner displays more, not less, emotion than you do. JoAnn shared:

I was absolutely numb . . . in a quasi state of shock. I didn't cry . . . I couldn't speak . . . I felt as though I was having an out-of-body experience. My husband, on the other hand, was sobbing uncontrollably, which was not only a first . . . but the *one and only* time he cried within all our years of marriage (thirteen years). I wasn't even moved to console him, which was very out of character for me.

After his and his wife's miscarriage, Daniel Grossoehme, the director of pastoral care at a children's hospital in Ohio, published part of his own journal to help shed some light on the experience of the father:

The Day

On Father's Day? Is this some sort of cruel joke?

On Sunday, the feast of the resurrection? The day drips with irony.

6:03 a.m.—as soon as I feel the tapping on my shoulder and open my eyes to see her standing next to me, I know.

Why can't the hospital have an OB department for this and not have us go to Labor and Delivery? Or why can't the Emergency Department have an ultrasound and get the OB resident there? I don't want to be in L & D!

Everyone is so calm and nice at the hospital. I just read an article at 4 o'clock Friday afternoon before I left an angry woman about pastoral care and miscarriage. More irony.

Tissue. Not fetus, not conceptus, but "tissue."

What do we do now? Just unceremoniously walk out? The nurse, the sleepy soft-spoken resident are gone, and the phlebotomist is just marking the vial from the blood draw. We just walk out holding hands.

Quiet. Subdued. A good word, that. Some tears—why can't I cry more? Am I normal? Hugs. "Let's stick close today." Reading the Sunday paper with tea at 9:30 a.m.—when was the last time we did *that*?

Standing in front of the toilet the resident said we could flush, we wave, we say good-bye using the names we'd chosen. I make the sign of the cross. "Lots of hugs."

"Do they think I'm a hysterical woman?" "Do they believe that I really was pregnant?" Self-doubt. No, they took you seriously. Remember the warning signs in the book? You had two. "So we did the right thing?" We did the right thing. Now what? More waiting to talk to the doctor about a follow-up visit. Knowing probable reasons doesn't help much. "Don't feel abandoned because I'm napping." Don't feel abandoned because I'm doing some chores. Both worried about abandoning the other. Napping on the couch. Subdued.[3]

Pregnancy loss affects men profoundly, although differently from the ways in which it may affect their partners. And men often feel the added burden of managing their own grief largely unsupported so they can support their spouses.

What were helpful ways couples found to keep their marriage relationship functioning during this difficult time? One of the primary guidelines is for each partner to do his or her best to acknowledge and respect the other person's needs. If the woman is at a point where she needs to talk endlessly about the loss, then her partner needs to find a way to listen. If the man is dealing with anger and denial, his spouse should not try to force him to talk. LeAnn said, "Something . . . that helped me was writing letters to my husband. He would always write back with love and encouragement." This can be a wonderful way for partners to reconnect. The distance that the letter provides can help men who feel helpless or incompetent in the face of expressed emotions, and writing back can offer them something concrete to do, something they know will be perceived as supportive by their wife. Some women talked about simple time spent with their husbands, especially during the week after the miscarriage—playing Jenga, reading together, going to movies, doing mindless things. If a woman needs periods of distraction amid periods of reflection, her spouse can be sensitive to her current need and help provide those distractions. Taking over household tasks that the woman usually does is a small but concrete action that can feel very supportive. Perhaps a husband could plan to set aside time every day for as much as a month to check in with his wife, and plan to listen. And perhaps wives could find direct, clear ways of reassuring their husbands that they are, in fact, being supportive and helpful. Women may need to encourage their partners to spend time with their own close friends or to talk to a pastor to find the support they need as well.

GRANDPARENTS

The loss is complicated for your own parents as well. They are grieving the loss of their hopes and dreams and delight over the baby that almost was, but they often also are grieving because of their own child's pain. Many grandparents I've spoken to recall feeling extraordinarily helpless. They want to do something to make things better but have no idea what to do or to say. Like many parents, they may want to fix what is hurting their own child and in so doing unwittingly devalue or fail to understand the grief of the parents who have lost their unborn baby.

Some women may discover for the first time that their own mother or grandmother experienced miscarriages. This can be comforting, if it leads the female family member to be empathetic and sensitive. It can also be very difficult, if the female family member failed to grieve her own loss well and comes out with something like, "I got over it; you should too." Others may find that their own miscarriage brings up painful memories for their parents or grandparents. One woman's 87-year-old grandmother cried when telling her about the miscarriage of her fourth pregnancy (after three live births), which had occurred almost sixty years before.

Grandparents often desperately desire something to do to make things better. Their efforts may feel loving or may feel like an attack on the grief. And again, relationships that were stressed prior to the loss may be in deep trouble afterward. One woman shared how difficult it was to work through the miscarriage with her parents:

> My parents are divorced. My dad and I are pretty close but [he] didn't want to know too much about the gynecological aspects. He was so sad. He wanted a grandchild so badly and he knew how much we wanted a child. My mother['s] and [my] relationship has always been strained and this did not bring us closer. She wanted it to, but it didn't. She was angry that I wouldn't let her take me to get my second surgery and didn't talk to me for a while.

As this story illustrates, it may be difficult for parents to accept a support role that is less active than what they might imagine or desire. Alternatively, some women and men may wish that their parents would do more to respond with support and comfort.

OTHER CHILDREN

A miscarriage is complicated when there are older children in the family. If they were not aware that their family was expanding, they may be confused and frightened by the unexplained and intense emotions that go along with grief. If they knew that they were going to be a big brother or big sister, they may have trouble understanding why this is no longer the case. For many children, it may be their first brush with death, and that can be a difficult thing to navigate, especially when the parents are dealing with their own powerful and complicated emotions.

Some parents will have already taken older children to see ultrasounds of their baby brother or sister (although some doctors' offices do not allow this practice). Molly recalled discovering at the ultrasound appointment that their fifteen-week-old boy had died. She said, "I hope my daughter who was there along with my husband will not ever remember the sobbing face of her mother at that moment." LeAnn, on the other hand, said, "I think that now I regret not having told our children about the loss of the other baby. At that time, I thought I was saving them from unnecessary grief. Instead, I am sure they wondered what was wrong with me for so long." Children are very sensitive to the emotional state of the adults in their lives, and older children can imagine all sorts of frightening reasons for emotional upset. Sometimes it can be better for them to have a concrete reason for displays of grief, rather than making up reasons for it on their own.

It can also be difficult to help older children understand a miscarriage because often they don't really understand pregnancy (although we adults understand much less than we imagine, don't we?). "There's a baby in mommy's tummy," we often tell them, "and you're going to be a big sister!" But what to say when the baby is gone and the child is no longer going to have a new status? It is important that you help your children understand that the loss had nothing to do with them. Children are developmentally egocentric and may easily imagine that the loss of the baby was somehow their fault, especially if they did not really want a younger sibling or had been having other behavior challenges. An example of how to tell a three-year-old about a miscarriage might be: "Honey, the baby in mama's tummy has died." (Use whatever phrases or words you have been using up to this point. It is best not to use euphemisms for death, especially phrases like "fallen asleep" or "passed away," as children are concrete thinkers and may not understand the difference between what they do at night when they fall asleep and what has happened to the baby.) "Mommy and Daddy are very sad. It is all right for you to talk to us about this. We want you to know that even if you see us crying or upset, we are not upset with you." It can be helpful to involve your children in concrete remembrances or memorial acts, which we will talk about more in chapter 13.

Don't be surprised if your older child responds to the news of the miscarriage in compassionate and caring ways. Children are often sensitive ministers to the people they love, especially when they do not get confused and imagine that they have caused the hurt their loved one is experiencing. Alternatively, don't be surprised if your older child either seems to not respond at all or responds by acting out for a time. Just like adults, children process difficult things very differently, but children do not have many cognitive and narrative tools to do that processing. A child who doesn't seem to respond may not have understood the fact of the pregnancy very well in the first place or may need time to let the news filter in. A child who throws tantrums for a week may be experiencing confusing emotions or may want to test to make sure that his parents still love him despite the grief over this bewildering event, even if he behaves badly. Never be afraid to seek help from a good children's counselor if you sense that your child may need assistance processing the family's loss or if you would appreciate expert guidance in helping your child understand the sad news. Seek help from a good counselor in general if you sense that your own emotional state may be affecting your family in serious ways.

INCORPORATING THE LOSS
INTO THE FAMILY NARRATIVE

It can be awkward to figure out ways of understanding yourselves as a family after a miscarriage. If you have no other children, you and your partner will have to find a new way of understanding yourselves as mother and father. Keep in mind that studies indicate that pregnancy loss when there is no living child has the potential to carry with it longer-lasting grief responses.[4] You may feel very much like a bereaved parent, but to outsiders you'll look like a couple with no children. Whether or not you have other children, you may not know what to say when people ask how many children you have. Is it right to say, "We had three children, two living"? Or "Two children; we had a miscarriage"? Or simply "We have two children"? Discovering ways to tell the story of your family that feel truthful to you will be important. Many families have developed rituals to mark the losses within their own family story. We'll talk about that more later, but for now keep in mind that having regular ways of incorporating the loss into your own narrative can be healing.

CLOSE FRIENDS

Your closest friends can be an important and strong source of support, but they can also be sources of additional pain. Relationships with friends can become complicated if those friends have children or are pregnant at the time of your miscarriage. It can be hard to know how to handle the existing love of that relationship when envy and resentment suddenly pop up, and you may not want to see or talk to some of your friends. I remember making some excuse to leave a dinner party early, full to the bitter brim of hearing my good friends swapping stories about their small children. Even people who care about us most may say things that hurt us or may fail to understand the depth of our grief. We will address some of this complicated territory in the next chapter, but for now, it can help to remember that friends who love you and who are emotionally healthy will want to support you and will welcome your advice on how best to offer that support. Don't be afraid to ask a friend to do shopping for you, to provide a meal, to help care for older children, to come sit and listen to you tell the story of what has happened to you. Be clear about your needs; if you don't want advice or feedback, say that up front. You might say, "I really need someone to talk to, someone who will just listen to me without saying anything at all. Could you please come over sometime this week and bring some bread and cheese and chocolate?" Also, remember that you have the right to ask friends to wait before coming to see you or talking to you about the loss.

Pregnancy loss, because it is exquisitely personal and painful, is a difficult grief to experience in communities of love and friendship. But while living through it, you urgently need the support of those people who care about you, even while they are experiencing grief as well. I pray that God will use your relational ties to undergird you and to remind you of God's love and care in the time of your loss.

REFLECTION QUESTIONS

1. How did your miscarriage affect your closest relationships?
2. How do you see your miscarriage affecting those relationships as you move into the future? If you imagine negative impacts, what are steps you might take to move toward healing?

EXERCISE

Write your partner a letter expressing whatever you want him to know. Include thanks for at least one way your partner has been supportive of you. Ask if he would be willing to write you a letter in response.

Chapter 10

Breaking the News

I scooted down the long row of chairs, settling in my usual spot toward the back. Often I liked to sit up front, but in that particular class I preferred to stay inconspicuous. I usually sat with a friend who we all knew would be a terrific pastor. He had a fantastic new Mac laptop and used to amuse himself during slow lectures by experimenting with the graphics on various photos. He greeted me that first day I showed up after the miscarriage, "Hey, how's it going?"

"Fine," I said. I shuffled my low-tech binder about for a minute and found the pen I wanted to use, then opened to a blank page and began to doodle. "Well, actually. We had a pretty awful week. I was pregnant." At that he looked up from the computer, confused. I realized I had started all wrong and wished I could take it back, but continued desperately, "We hadn't told many people yet, so most people didn't know . . . but I had a miscarriage last week."

My friend looked blank. "I'm so sorry," he said. "Um . . . how far along were you?"

I did what I had been doing all week, apologetically saying, "Only seven weeks." My use of that ridiculous word "only" set up the poor guy for disaster. Taking my lead, he said, "Well, it's good that you weren't very far along. And you and Chris are young . . . you have plenty of time." He waited to see if I would say anything else, smiled sympathetically, and looked back at the computer screen.

"Yeah." I sat there the rest of class and didn't hear a word, trying to figure out why I was so angry. Over the next hours, as I compulsively shared the news with people I bumped into, I heard the whole list of platitudes. "There was probably something wrong, so it's God's way of taking care of things." "Well, the timing just wasn't right, I guess." "It's good to know you can get pregnant so easily." "God has a plan." "Were you guys *trying* to get pregnant?"—this last in an incredulous tone of voice. With every conversation I became more and more furious, more and more miserable. Was *everyone* going to make me feel like I was overreacting? Did *anyone* get the fact that I wanted *that baby*, not just "a baby"? And were all these people seriously going to be pastors?

I walked into the last class of the afternoon, close to tears, and stopped to talk to a woman named Amy. I knew Amy as a good acquaintance, but we weren't close friends. She could tell, however, that I was upset and asked how I was. I looked straight at her as the preclass shuffle began around us, and I said, "I am horrible. I had a miscarriage last week." As people moved into their places, I blurted out too many details, whispering fiercely, "I walked around bleeding all last week. And Amy, you remember the eschatology class we had together—all I can think about is the baby's body. Which toilet did I flush my child down? I don't even know where I lost her."

I was embarrassed that I'd spilled something so personal to someone I barely knew, and especially because it happened as everyone was quieting down, ready for the lecture to begin. It felt as though I'd committed an extremely ugly breach of protocol. I got ready to dive for my seat, ready to gather my protective fury back around me.

But Amy just looked at me. Tears suddenly filled her eyes as she whispered, "Oh, God." She held my gaze for a moment more, and I could see in her tears the reflection of my own grief and horror at what had happened. She said softly, "I am so sorry." She touched my shoulder and we stood like that for a short minute, and then we sat down. Rather, she sat down. I fled for the bathroom, as I was doing so often, and I wept. But this time was different. Instead of the burning, maddened tears I had spilled all week, these tears were cooling. I felt for the first time since the miscarriage that Jesus was no longer absent. I felt as if God had showed God's face for the very first time, as if God's own face was streaked with tears of compassion and grief and empathy.

That moment was the first and only moment I sensed God's presence for quite some time—months, in fact. But I clung to it. And it came through the willingness of another Christian to open herself to understand what I was feeling, to allow herself to be affected by my pain. Six words. I will never again underestimate the healing power of six words.

Neither, however, will I ever again underestimate the power of thoughtless words to wound. Words trickle out of us to hide our discomfort, to mask pain and make sadness go away. And the painful, thoughtless things people said were often absolutely appalling.

Why is it so difficult to talk about miscarriage? Why did the words about my own experience catch in my throat? Why was it that well-intentioned people who genuinely wanted to show me compassion and care found it so hard to say anything helpful? First, I believe it has to do with the fact that talking about miscarriage necessarily means we have to talk about our bodies' reproductive parts. Most women have mastered the art of invisibly palming tampons, and we don't like to mention a bleeding uterus, even when it's our normal monthly cycle. We are uncomfortable sharing information about that extremely private part of us, and there's some sense in which we're ashamed of it, too. Second, our culture's general apprehension about death is compounded further by a miscarriage. Somehow it doesn't seem either comfortable or politically correct to use the term "death" in the same breath as "pregnancy." We have a pleasant illusion that modern medicine can fix just about anything, and we're not sure how to talk about a pregnancy that fails, that ends in death and disappointment. It is far easier to minimize the loss—to fence it around with words that will make it seem less painful, less important—than it is to enter into a space occupied by a messy, complicated grief. Finally, because miscarriage isn't talked about, many people have never experienced this kind of loss or known of it in another's life, so they respond lightly out of true ignorance, having no idea of the real pain that accompanies a pregnancy loss.

This chapter will talk about breaking the news to other people: the people outside that closest inner circle of immediate family and friends who may have already known about your pregnancy and will need to be informed about your miscarriage, and the people who did not know about your pregnancy but who need to know that you will be grieving for a time. We'll hear from other women to find out what helpful things people did and said to them. Hopefully these stories will give you some concrete ways to make the painful process of sharing the news of your loss a little easier to bear.

The way you break the news will depend somewhat on the extent to which you had let people know about your pregnancy. Ironically, those of us who avoid sharing the news until the end of that statistically magical first trimester may end up with less support than we need. Katherine shared her experience:

> I had surgery after both deaths, since I was unable to deliver the babies due to a cervical issue. I went back to work almost immediately, in order to keep myself busy. I felt very alone and isolated. When we were pregnant with our first son, we had told everyone we were pregnant . . . and I found people were more invested in what we were going through. Whereas, with our second son, we decided not to tell anyone until the third month. It was much harder having to call people and tell them that we had been pregnant

again and lost another child. People did not know what to say, so they said very little. I felt like I had no one to talk to during that horrible time and it was one of the lowest points in my life.

If fewer people know, you may find yourself in the painful position of grieving something that feels profoundly unreal. When the community is unaware of the loss, it can feel imaginary. Susan said, "We had only told our families and a few close friends about the pregnancy, but somehow I felt like a liar, like I had lied about being pregnant. It sounds ridiculous, I know, but that's how I felt." When our experience is not mirrored in the lives of those around us, we may end up with a painful conflict between our own reality and others' recognition (or lack thereof) of that reality.

Many of us, on the other hand, have shared the good news far and wide. If it is our first pregnancy or if we've had other successful pregnancies, or if we have not been close to someone who has experienced a miscarriage, we may not imagine any reason not to tell our co-workers, our Facebook friends, our book club, and the nice checkout lady at the grocery store that we're expecting. The joy is great, and we love to share great news.

However, fast-forward to the week after the pregnancy ends. You run to the grocery, wearing your glasses and sweatpants, puffy-eyed and miserable, to replenish your stock of ibuprofen and ice cream. You wind up in a long line of people, and you suddenly realize that you are going to be checking out with that same nice woman. She sees you and her face lights up. "Still dealing with that nasty morning sickness, honey?" Misery. You mumble, "Um, no, I had a miscarriage," and see her face change. The line is too long, the moment too awkward, and after saying, "Oh, that's too bad, but you'll be pregnant again soon," she sweeps your purchases into a bag and you run home to hide.

I wish I could tell you that there is a way to completely avoid situations like this, a special trick to ensure that every time you break the news your heart will be protected and people will respond with sensitivity. But no such trick exists. However, being proactive in sharing the news with other people can help you avoid repeating over and over again that moment when someone goes from jolly congratulations to embarrassed retreat. If your spouse, your mother, or your best friend wants a concrete way to help you, inviting them to help with this process of news breaking can provide them with an ideal opportunity to be supportive.

Telling the people who knew of your pregnancy directly rather than letting them find out by accident will always help both you and them handle the ensuing conversations. Many people are most comfortable doing this via e-mail or even their social networking site. The advantages of doing it electronically are (1) you can write one message that says what you want it to say and be finished quickly, (2) you give other people a chance to think carefully about their response, and (3) you can protect yourself from unhelpful interaction while the loss is fresh. This can be an especially good choice if you need to notify a large group of people with whom you are not especially close, like an office full of co-workers. The disadvantages of online communication, on the other hand, are (1) it puts another layer of distance between you and the very people who might be sources of deep support for you, (2) if you write a message in which you share more than you want, or accidentally communicate a tone or an emotion you regret, the message lives on in original detail, and (3) you run the risk of accidentally including extra contacts or forgetting to include persons, as well as having the message forwarded indiscriminately.

Let's imagine that you had shared your pregnancy with your boss, since your doctor's appointments would need to happen during work hours. Even though you asked her to keep it quiet for a while, she misunderstood and joyfully announced your news at a staff meeting. This was slightly annoying, but as long as you were pregnant, it didn't seem like such a big deal. Your co-workers were happy for you, and it was kind of fun having people ask questions about the baby-to-be and interesting to hear their stories about their own pregnancies or wives' pregnancies.

But over the following weekend, you miscarry at nine weeks. You need to take a few days off from work, and you are dreading going back to the office. You *really* don't want to talk about it with your co-workers, and you are getting sufficient support at home. You are also intensely resentful of your boss for sharing your news too early. This might be a good opportunity for a group e-mail. In the e-mail, communicate clearly what you want from the recipients. Do you want them to offer support? Do you want them to ask you how you're doing? Do you want them to pretend it never happened? Some may not respect your wishes, but if you don't communicate what those wishes are, people will respond in a wild variety of ways, all trying to do what they think you would want them to do. An example of an e-mail sent in this situation might look like this:

To: Employees of Smith, Johnson & Marks [double-check to make absolutely sure your list is correct]:

Subject: Sad news (or "Pregnancy")

Dear friends,

Most of you knew that Chris and I were expecting a baby. Sadly, I had a miscarriage this weekend. I will be returning to work next week. I would strongly prefer not to talk about our loss at work; please just act normally around me. Chris and I have plenty of loving support and we are grateful for your good wishes. If you would like to do something, it would please us if you made a contribution to the March of Dimes.

Thank you,

Elise

Letting closer friends know by phone or in person can be very healing, but it can also be painful if people you are close to respond in ways that feel hurtful. You will have to decide. If you do not feel up to the interaction, ask for help from someone who loves you. Many partners would be grateful for something specific and helpful to do, something they know will be supportive. If you are able, be clear about what would help you. The people who care about you are likely to say something like, "What can I do?" or "I wish there was some way I could help." You or your partner could ask for them to bring over a meal or to spend some special time with any other children you have.

What are other responses grieving families found helpful or healing? Katherine said, "I appreciated the cards people sent (though I never received any cards after our second son died, which was devastating)." "Neighbors and girlfriends brought food, etc.," remembered Molly. Mary shared about her good friend "Jane," who had also had fertility problems. She said, "To this day, 'Jane' is still very supportive. She is one of the few mothers I can stand and not feel horribly inadequate around. She also doesn't judge me when I am angry that others have babies and I don't. She supports me without feeding my self-pity. With her, we talk about it, just for a while, and then we move on to talk about our favorite TV shows, our friends, or what we're going to [do] next." Christine listed "hugs; listening; sharing their stories of loss; being present" as helpful responses she'd received. Heather said, "Those who just listened were the most helpful, also those who cried with me. My friend who had three miscarriages came over, and we just sat and talked about God for a long time. The church music ministry sent a very sweet card with notes from everyone that were very appropriate. Another friend dropped everything and brought my favorite meal, and played with Noly [our older daughter]." And LeAnn shared:

> I loved the cards and letters that friends sent to me. Sometimes I dreaded seeing people or talking to a friend for the first time after the miscarriage because I knew I would end up trying to make that person

feel that everything was OK. It was also nice to have someone who would call other people with the news and take care of specific tasks for me. . . . Perhaps the most touching gesture came from our female pastor and friend. She wrote a simple note describing my tears as prayers to God on behalf of my children and enclosed a beautiful handkerchief with the note.

Like LeAnn, I was blessed by many of the responses of caring people who reached out to offer sympathy after our losses. I had asked Chris to keep our first miscarriage a secret from his churches. Well, the word got out (as it does in a small town) and, much to my surprise, I was glad. Many of the older women in the congregations, instead of offering platitudes, would hug me gently and say, "Sweetheart, I know it's hard. I lost my first baby and I didn't think I'd ever get over it. You just call if you need anything or if we can bring you some food." The churches sent flowers, and seeing them arrayed alongside the bouquets from our family was heart healing.

Circumstances were different after our next two miscarriages, which occurred very early in the pregnancies. My grief was different, and Chris and I were both serving large churches. We told only our closest friends, locally the pastors and friends we worked alongside. They blessed us by holding our secret at a time when it would have been oppressive to help a large congregation process our loss. They blessed us by bringing food. And one dear friend, who had had a miscarriage herself after my first one, brought a spa gift certificate and the brand of maxipads I'd specified over the phone. Greater love hath no one than the girl who will pick up your pads at the grocery store so you and your husband don't have to leave the house.

No matter how you do it, you will have to break the news. Being proactive, thinking carefully about your own needs, and communicating clearly those needs to those around you can open doors for people to respond as they truly want to: with compassion, sympathy, and care.

REFLECTION QUESTIONS

1. Whom did you have the most difficult time telling about your loss (or whom do you most dread telling, if you have not yet broken the news)? Why?
2. Did you keep your pregnancy a secret, or did you tell people you were expecting? Do you regret that decision, or are you glad? Why?

EXERCISE

Think about one specific way you wish someone would minister to you or care for you. (This could be anything, including providing a meal, going out for coffee with you, watching older children for a couple of hours, or heading out to a state park for a walk and talk.) Now ask the person of your choice if they would care for you in that way.

Chapter 11

When Other People Say Hurtful Things

*A*fter you've broken the news to your acquaintances, what happens next? We've talked about some helpful responses people may offer to your loss, but many people will say things that hurt deeply. In this chapter we will go through several of the most common of these comments that many women find hurtful. We'll also talk about *why* these words hurt. At the end of the discussion of each comment, a sample conversation includes a suggestion for responding to the comment.

As you read these comments and as you enter into these conversations in real life, it can help to remember that most of the time, people are not being intentionally cruel or uncaring. They are fumbling to find something kind to say, confronted with a loss they may not understand or be comfortable imagining. Alternatively, they may be saying exactly what would help them in a similar situation. I have been surprised over and over again to hear that comments that put me over the boiling point during my own season of grief were very comforting to other women. However, in the midst of your own pain, the last thing you need is to be placed in the role of miscarriage grief educator. This is why it can help to have some prepared responses for these common comments so that you don't have to respond out of your own fragile emotions. And it is always fine to simply say, "Thank you for your concern," and walk away, if you need to protect yourself from further interaction.

The sample responses I offer will do three things: (1) communicate to the individuals that you believe they have good intentions and are trying to be kind, (2) indicate gently that their comment was either inaccurate or hurtful, and (3) offer them a helpful alternative response while providing you with a chance to either close or continue the conversation.

"YOU'LL HAVE ANOTHER BABY"

Katherine remembered, "Many people said . . . that I could always have another baby—not very reassuring when you have lost two . . . and babies/souls are not interchangeable, in my opinion." This is one of the most often-heard responses. Sometimes it comes out as "Well, you're young and healthy" or "You and your wife have plenty of time." No matter how it's stated, the unspoken message is that grief over a *particular* baby, a *particular* loss, should not be the issue. The assumption is that what you've actually lost is only one of many chances to be pregnant. LeAnn said, "One of the most hurtful things that people said to me over and over again was that there would be other babies. Well, I wanted *that* baby. The baby I had prayed for, longed to hold, dreamed about."

On a vastly different scale, this is a lot like telling someone who's just had to put their beloved dog to sleep, "Well, you can always buy another dog." The problem is that in that moment, the person is not sad about dogs in general or the loss of being a person with a dog. They are grieving that particular friend, the one they named and kennel-trained and walked every day, the one with the two different-colored eyes and the birthday in June and the bad habit of chewing the doorstop. The same is true with miscarriage. "You'll have more children" assumes that you are sad because you have been stalled in your journey to become a person with a child. But by and large, although the loss of that dream for that time is indeed a component of the grief of miscarriage, you are mourning the loss of a particular baby-to-be. You are mourning that particular little one, the one who was conceived during a stressful time at work and came as a bright ray of sunshine into a gray winter, the one for whom you were eating differently and saving money and fingering baby blankets at the mall, the one who was going to be arriving in August and having a birthday at the same time as your beloved deceased grandfather, the one who might have had your husband's dimple or your dark hair. Now you will never know those things, never meet the one who was changing your body so dramatically, and you are mourning that *particular* little one.

Furthermore, "you'll have more children" makes some completely unwarranted assumptions about your and your partner's history. This is an inappropriate thing to say to a couple who has no known reproductive challenges; it is an excruciatingly painful thing to say to a couple who has struggled with infertility, perhaps for years, or who has just suffered one of many sequential miscarriages.

So what to say to this comment? You will find your own comfort zone in responding, but a conversation might go like this:

"Oh honey, that's too bad, but you and your husband are young, you'll have more children."

"Thank you for trying to be kind. I know you are intending to give us hope. Perhaps we will be able to have another child, but right now we are sad because we have lost this particular child. We would appreciate your prayers."

"THE BABY MUST HAVE HAD SOMETHING WRONG WITH IT"

LeAnn shared, "Someone said to me that this was God's way of taking care of a baby that had something wrong with it. Well, that may have been true, but that comment did not make me feel any better." This is an especially loaded thing to say. In our culture, many people think that to have a child with something "wrong with it" would be a tragedy of the first magnitude. Although comprehensive statistics are hard to come by, the majority of parents who discover they are carrying a child with Down syndrome choose to have an abortion,[1] and we have the option to voluntarily "get rid of" fetuses that prenatal screening seems to indicate are compromised with birth defects. Many people assume that nonperfect babies are better off dead before they complicate their parents' lives. Someone was just that direct with Heather, asking incredulously, "You wouldn't want a baby that had something wrong with it, would you?"

There are three assumptions here. First, this response assumes that the parents of the lost fetus would be only too glad to be freed from the dependent life of a child with special needs. And some, in fact, would. No one hopes that their child will have spina bifida or cystic fibrosis or Down syndrome, and most expectant parents feel ill-equipped to deal with challenges like this. This is why, for some women, this comment does in fact feel helpful. Nonetheless, despite the extra difficulties, most parents of children with special needs want them and love them dearly. And especially for Christians, the life of a child, even a child who bears special physical or developmental challenges, is exceedingly precious, and its end is no more desirable than the end of the life of a child who is physically "whole."

The second assumption is this: no one should grieve the end of the life of a child who is so severely compromised developmentally that she or he would not be able to survive. I find this curious. Certainly, if the child's life is going to be unsustainable, it will end, and there is a sense in which it is easier to bear physically (both for the mother and for the developing child) the earlier the development ceases. However, parents would be expected to grieve the loss of a child born with wrongly developed internal organs. Parents would be expected to grieve the loss of a child born with a terminal illness or with no brain function. Why, then, would a pregnancy that ended early for such reasons be a source of no pain at all? A parent could legitimately *prefer* that unsustainable development cease sooner rather than later, for the sake of that child and for the sake of the mother's health, and *still* grieve that the unborn child they loved was so afflicted physically that she could not survive.

The third assumption this comment makes is that the pregnancy ended because of a developmental issue with the child. Well, perhaps it did; many do. But perhaps it didn't. There is no way for the person making that comment to know.

How might you respond to this comment?

"You wouldn't want a baby that had something wrong with it, would you? This is God's way of taking care of babies that have something wrong with them."

"I can tell that you are trying to be helpful. Thank you. We may never know why this happened, whether or not there was something physically wrong with the baby. But we are sad that this little one will not be part of our lives. We would appreciate your prayers."

"THIS IS FOR THE BEST." "IT'S GOD'S TIMING." "LOOK ON THE BRIGHT SIDE."

Heather kept hearing, "It's for the best. . . . It just wasn't meant to be." Another way people say the same thing is to make comments about "God's perfect will," saying, "God's time is best." The assumption here is that this person has some way of knowing that your miscarriage was the will of God. The logical implication is that you ought to be glad about it, rather than grieving; that a person of *faith* would accept or rejoice in the loss rather than mourning what clearly came from God's hands. For people who believe that there is a good purpose for the loss, this idea can be healing. However, this sort of comment can alternatively make you both resent God and feel as if your own faith is somehow lacking. Mary shared her frustration with these sorts of responses:

> The cruelest thing anyone could say is that "it happened for a reason" or "this is supposed to teach you something." I feel like saying, "You go and rack up some misery and then you can tell me that I *deserved* it. . . . I am

willing to concede that miscarriages happen because the baby might not be healthy and would not have made it anyway. I'm OK with that, I accept that. But I sure as hell didn't deserve it.

My baby was due around Christmastime. My birthday is on Christmas as well, thus my name, Mary. My mother, grandmother, and I were sitting around a table making Christmas cookies, as per our tradition, and in passing I said I wish we were making a birthday cake for a baby instead. My grandmother said, "Well, think about how much money you saved."

As exemplified by Mary's grandmother, another common riff on this theme is "Look on the bright side." People going here often start their sentences with "At least . . ." "At least it was early." "At least you won't have to deal with that morning sickness anymore." "At least you already have one child." Or, as Heather recalled, "After I lost Payton, someone said, 'How are you?' I said, 'Not great.' She said, 'Well, at least you can have children. You should be thankful for what you already have.'" This is a little like saying, "Your husband died? Well, at least you have a nice house. You should be thankful for that." The unspoken assumption is that a particular loss should not grieve you, because you have other (perhaps related, perhaps not) positive things in your life.

Very often, people who say these things are reacting out of their own places of brokenness. Women who are secretly lugging around the unrelenting frustration and grief of infertility often will react out of their own pain, rather than being able to sympathize with your loss. They think, "If I could only get pregnant, if I only knew that I *could* have children, it would be such a gift!" And so they react out of their longing and envy, hurting too much themselves to be able to open themselves to your pain. Of course, this doesn't make these comments any easier to hear.

A conversation might be:

"Well, I'm sure it's for the best—God's timing is perfect, after all. And at least you know you can get pregnant."

"Thank you for trying to be kind. We are glad we can get pregnant, but we are extremely sad that we lost our baby. We need God's comfort right now, and we hope you'll pray for us."

"DID IT HAPPEN BECAUSE . . . ?"

This is perhaps the most offensive way people can respond. In our culture, we think that every event has some sort of easily discoverable scientific cause. Many people have heard snippets of research or folktales about pregnancy and miscarriage and are only too glad to help you categorize cause and effect for your own loss. Some people do this to assuage their own discomfort. It is far easier to talk about a specific cause of an uncomfortable loss than to sit and suffer with a grieving person who has no reasons, no place to rest the blame. As we have discussed elsewhere, there is often no way of medically figuring out why the loss occurred. But most women, because the loss happens in their own bodies, because they have spent weeks or months doing specific things to keep the baby healthy, and because their own grief leads so easily into guilt, are already flagellating themselves for actions or situations they've imagined might have affected their pregnancies. Even the word "*mis*carriage" seems to imply that she is to blame, that she has failed to carry her baby to term. Having an outsider offer another reason for the loss, especially a reason that could be construed as the mother's fault, can be both infuriating and horribly guilt-inducing.

A classic example of this is the question Heather received: "Did it happen because you are so skinny?" Or, what I heard from someone, "I bet it happened because you are so stressed out." This implies two things: there was a reason for this, and it was a reason that you could have done something about. It is hard to imagine a more insensitive response. Debbie received one, however: "I actually talked to a Methodist minister after the tubal pregnancy over my—I guess at the time it was depression, and he asked me if I had ever had an abortion. Needless to say I never talked to him about it again."

Sadly, these accusatory responses to a woman's deep grief are not uncommon. "It must have been your fault" is the unspoken assumption. Bereaved women are already struggling against blaming themselves. An accusatory response offered by an outsider only makes things worse.

What might you say in this case? You will have responses that match your own temperament, responses that fit with the relationship you have with the questioner. It may be that you simply want to say, "What an offensive, hurtful thing to say!" and walk off. But if you feel that the person is attempting to be caring, you could try something like this:

"Did it happen because you're so skinny?"

"No, it did not. I know you are trying to be kind, and I appreciate your intentions. But when you asked that question, I felt like you were saying that this was my fault. We don't know why this happened. Doctors never determine a reason for most miscarriages, and they occur to women of all shapes and sizes. We are very sad and we would be glad to have your prayers."

"HERE'S WHAT YOU SHOULD DO"

Heather, who struggled with fertility challenges and recurrent miscarriages, heard a lot of these kinds of comments. People said to her, "Maybe you should just stop trying and adopt" and "If you adopt, you'll get pregnant right away; everybody does." Other people may trot out the natural remedies for miscarriage they've read about online or say things like, "Well, my sister-in-law's cousin had all these miscarriages until they just quit stressing about it so much." There are two major problems with this response. First, as we mentioned before, it assumes that the unique loss of that particular pregnancy is nothing more than a failure in the baby production process, only worth grieving insofar as it's a bump on the road to producing a baby. If the baby making is "fixed," the sadness will go away. This is not inevitably true. Many women are grieving the loss of that *particular* unborn child, not solely another setback (although some experience it that way as well). The second problem is that, again, it implies that there is an easy fix for the loss, which means that the mother or father could have used the easy miracle cure that's being propounded to prevent it—which means that, again, the loss is their fault.

A final word about adoption. While many people have known situations in which a family struggling with childbearing adopted a child and then gave birth to a child, this is *never* an appropriate response to throw out in casual conversation, nor is it a healing response to someone's pregnancy loss. Again, it's a lot like saying "you'll have more kids," in that it assumes that there is no need to grieve for *this* lost little one. And adoption is *never* a magic bullet to be deployed in the quest for birth children. God calls some families to enlarge by adoption, just as the family of God is enlarged by adoption, and it can be one of the most rich and deep blessings human beings experience, both for the adoptive family and for the adopted child. However, it is heartbreaking to think of a child being adopted not because she is desired and beloved, but because her new parents hope that she'll fix their infertility problems. The conversation about adoption is one to be held among close friends and family, seeking to discern God's leading on a particular path, not a miracle cure to be tossed out in hopes of a quick resolution to someone else's pain.

How, then, to respond?

"My brother and his wife adopted and then got pregnant. You should think about doing that."

"Thank you for wanting to be helpful. We are grieving the ending of this particular child's life. We will keep listening for God to lead us in the right direction, but for now, we are simply hurting as we process this loss. Thank you for praying for us."

NO RESPONSE

Christine talked about the difficulty of people responding with "ambiguity . . . averting their eyes as I passed." Sometimes there may be no response at all, and this is often as hard to deal with as responses that are hurtful. Molly said:

> My family was far away. I received calls from Florida friends and family, but my little sister (in her defense, she is eight years younger and we were never really close) never called or even mentioned it. At the time I was incredulous that she would not even send a note or even a quick "Hey, I'm sorry about what happened" when we would visit Florida. I have learned a very basic, but important lesson from this: You simply can't have the same expectations of all people. I suppose some people don't know what to say at a time like this so they say nothing. *Something* is still better than no acknowledgment at all.

Whether people respond with actively hurtful comments or they hurt you by seeming to ignore your loss, the final goal is to find a way to keep those hurtful comments and silences at arm's length. It's easier said than done, but as a friend of ours is fond of saying, "Don't let them live rent-free in your head." Do what you can to replay comforting things people have said more often than you chew on the painful comments. When you can't quit nursing something painful someone said, talk it over with someone you trust to listen. Let them comfort you and be indignant on your behalf. Let loving words sink in more deeply than the thoughtless comments. Know that above all, God takes your pain seriously, God does not dismiss your loss, and God is reaching out to comfort and heal your broken heart.

REFLECTION QUESTIONS

1. What hurtful things did people say to you? Why do you think they hurt?
2. What helpful things did people say to you? Why do you think they helped?

EXERCISE

Close your eyes. Imagine that you are alone in a room with God. Let the silence settle in for a minute. What do you want God to say to you?

Chapter 12

Long-Term Effects

*F*our months after our first miscarriage, summer arrived, and I began clinical pastoral education. Required for ordination in our conference, summer CPE was an intensive twelve-week program hosted in a hospital system. Participants were divided into small groups and assigned to various clinical settings—nursing homes, hospitals, hospice units—to practice chaplaincy. Not only did we serve as chaplains in our settings throughout the Carolinas, but we also were subjected to one of the most intensive self-examinations of our lives. I was assigned to a large downtown hospital in Columbia, South Carolina. Rather than commute an hour and a half from home, I moved in with Chris's sister and her family for the summer, settling in for what I knew would be a tough experience.

I had always been uncomfortable in hospitals. I am introverted enough that knocking on someone's door in a hospital and going in to find a way to start a conversation with them and see if they needed pastoral care sounded like an absolute nightmare. And it was every bit as difficult as I'd feared. I was exhausted every day. It took an intense effort for me to enter room after room, trying to be a representative of God in situations of extreme anxiety, grief, or fear. As if that weren't enough, there was the challenge of the hours spent in IPR, Interpersonal Relations sessions, during which those of us going through the program learned to ask each other pointed and personal questions about our interaction with patients, trying to lay open the bruises and infections in our own lives so that they could be dealt with safely before they made us unfit ministers ten years down the road. I cried myself to sleep many nights. During my nights on call, I lay awake on a hospital bed smelling the odors of cancer treatment and the food I hadn't eaten.

We all were assigned special areas to patrol during regular days, although during on-call we were responsible for the whole hospital. My two areas were one of the cancer floors and—who would have guessed?—the "women's floor," where everything from labor and delivery to hysterectomies took place. This hospital had the only neonatal intensive care unit (NICU) in the area, so we had lots of high-risk pregnancies on that floor. It was full of women waiting to see what was going to happen, trying to make it to the thirtieth, or the thirty-second week.

I thought being on the women's floor would be awful for me, but I discovered I sort of liked it. Despite a tiny jab of envy every time I walked in to see a new baby and a radiant mother, it was still joyful, and I could still take pleasure in their happiness. I also felt as if God was using my own loss in some healing ways. It felt as if space had been carved out within me by my loss, and that was a space where I could receive other women's losses with empathy, even if the losses were quite different in nature. A couple had a stillbirth, and through my own tears, I anointed the cool, sweet head of their baby as we worshiped and committed the child's life to God. A woman on bed rest asked if I had any children. I answered that I didn't, then hesitated, and for some reason shared with her what I shared with no other patient the entire summer, that I had had a miscarriage. Her eyes shone as she said, "Oh, so did I—two of them. I didn't think anyone would understand how afraid I've been this time around. I want you to meet my husband, because you'll know how to pray for us."

I was also intensely angry sometimes, in ways I would not have been were it not for my miscarriage. I remember spending time every day for a week with a crack-addicted mother on bed rest to slow her pre-term labor. Like many addicts, she said she wanted to change things, but admitted to me that she probably wouldn't. When her baby was born, I stood in the NICU for half an hour, just gazing at him. He was big for a NICU baby, over six pounds, and looked healthy and beautiful, blond fuzz haloing his head. He was born crack-addicted and had some tremors, but was to all appearances perfect. And then they were gone, and I was overcome with fury. *That woman!* I fumed. *She is going to be back on drugs as soon as she leaves, and what is going to happen to her baby? I would take him! I would take that baby, and I would want him and love him!* A similar feeling swept me when I was called to the room of a woman who had asked to see a chaplain. She had no legs, suffered from raging diabetes, and was living with a man who had four other children and treated her as a maid, a man who had told her bluntly that he let her stay only because of the check she got from working at Walmart. She was in the grip of terrible depression and told me she didn't want her baby. I was profoundly sorry for her, and I listened to her and prayed with her and found social services folks to help care for her. But the whole time I was in her room, I couldn't keep my eyes from straying to her baby. As far away from his mother as possible, he kicked and slept and cried in his Plexiglas bassinet in the corner. She never looked at him, never picked him up. On one level, I understood. She was hurting too badly to care for someone else, and it made all the sense in the world. But again, everything inside me was screaming out, *Let me take your baby!*

Despite these challenges, I told myself that my emotions were perfectly normal. I felt as if I had dealt with my own grief thoroughly and was able to care for other people without inflicting my own issues on them.

This is why what happened toward the end of the summer was such a shock. We had been in the chapel for a memorial service when the on-call pager went off. My cancer floor, I saw, and I hurried to the cancer building. *Oh, brother*, was my first thought when I arrived. The patient in question was an on-again, off-again resident of the ward with lung cancer who drove everyone nuts. He was manipulative and irritable and spent most of his time trying to get the nurses or other staff people to buy him things out of the vending machines.

"What's going on?" I asked.

The harried nurse answered, "Oh, it's 'John.' He's dying. I've given him something to make him more comfortable and he should be asleep soon. Can you just go in there and talk to him?"

My comfort level had grown a lot since the first weeks, and I immediately headed for his door. I pushed it open and was appalled. The emaciated man was propped up in his bed, coughing, drowning in his blood. He held a small pink plastic basin under his mouth with trembling hands, spitting blood and mucus into it after every hack. I was frozen, both by his distress and by my fear. He looked up. "Hold this for me. I can't hold it anymore."

I reached out for the basin. Gingerly, I held it by the edge, close to his mouth. Then I grabbed a clean towel and used that instead. Blood was everywhere, in his teeth and on his chin, on his hands.

He did start to get calmer, though. He continued to cough, but he settled down on his pillow and just looked at me, wide-eyed. And something odd possessed me. I found myself overwhelmed with compassion for him, strange and deep tenderness. I took his hand and I started to sing. I sang "Amazing Grace," "Swing Low, Sweet Chariot," and "Be Thou My Vision," and every other hymn and lullaby I could think of. As I sang, he drifted to sleep. Shaking, I washed my hands and left. I heard later that afternoon that he had died without waking up again.

The next day was IPR, and I was responsible for presenting a verbatim, a case study of a hospital care experience. We were supposed to select cases that we knew we hadn't handled well, and because of my fumbling, frozen response when I had first walked into the room, John's death seemed like a natural choice to me. I wrote it up and presented it to my small group of peers and my supervisor. My peers asked some questions, and the conversation eventually reached a lull.

Then my supervisor looked at me and said, "Why did this bother you so much?" *What?* I thought. *I just watched a man drown in his own blood! What do you mean, why did it bother me?* "Um . . . the choking was disturbing . . . he never woke up again. . . ." He waved this away. "No, there's something else," he insisted. He thought a moment, and then said, "The blood. When was the last time you saw this much blood?"

"Blood?" He didn't know what he was talking about, I internally muttered. I'd never seen that much . . . *oh.* "I guess it was . . . when my baby died," I said. And then I burst into tears and couldn't stop crying. To this point I'd been very self-protective in these sessions. I had carefully revealed enough "issues" to give the group something to work on, but I had not shown much emotion. I was humiliated to lose control like this, but I couldn't stop. My head on my lap, my arms over my head, I sobbed until I was tired. After several moments, finally quieted, I reluctantly sat up to face my peers. Into the silence that stretched on and on, one eventually said, "You had told us about your miscarriage, but I had no idea it had affected you so much."

Neither had I.

Be prepared for your grief to rise up and ambush you, months or even years after you think you should be done working through it. LeAnn shared:

> My grief continues to show up even after two and a half years. Nearly two years after the last miscarriage, my husband and I had a night at home alone. We rented *Facing the Giants*, a Christian movie with a story line about a couple that has been unable to have a child. I became very angry during that movie and began to feel as if I had not had enough faith or prayed hard enough for my child. I know this is a movie that has touched many people, but somehow it stirred my grief, and all of those questions surfaced again. I also find myself not wanting to hold or fuss over babies as much as I did before the last miscarriage. I guess I am protecting myself from that desire to love a baby again.

Many related or unrelated events can be trigger points. For lots of women, seeing mothers who seem to be unloving or ungrateful parents is a strong trigger of their own grief. Tammy was surprised by her anger:

> I was in a store one day and saw a mother being so loud and angry with her infant for crying. The baby was clearly very sick and she was getting medicine for him, but his little cry was so faint. . . . She was yelling and

telling him to "shut up" and I lost it. . . . I called her out for treating him that way, and as you would imagine it ended up in a yelling match. The whole time I was thinking to myself that I lost two I really wanted, and it made me sick to see someone have a child and show no compassion or care. . . . I regret arguing with that lady today, but that was when I first realized that I had suppressed some negative feelings. . . . I suppose I will always feel those feelings.

You will never get over a significant loss. You will always have some feelings connected to your miscarriage; a loss like this changes a person forever. But it can help to be prepared for some of the particular ways you can expect to experience effects of your loss over the months and years to come.

THE FIRST SIX MONTHS

Your grief will be the most intense during the first half of a year following your loss. Several challenges can be part of those first months.

Anxiety

Some studies have shown that for any woman, but especially for women who have had prior struggles with anxiety disorders, a miscarriage can trigger episodes of obsessive-compulsive disorder (OCD) or post-traumatic stress disorder (PTSD). What might this look like? Anxiety in general may make you feel nervous, restless, tense, irritable, tired, or unable to concentrate or sleep.[1] These symptoms can show up both emotionally and physically. A screening more specifically for obsessions and compulsions might look for symptoms like "recurrent and persistent thoughts or images that [feel] intrusive and distressing, particularly in regard to the miscarriage, and/or . . . repetitive behaviors, such as hand washing or checking."[2] Symptoms of trauma could include intense, recurrent dreams or memories about the miscarriage that make you feel extremely afraid, helpless, or horror-struck; a general feeling of numbness and detachment; or intense distress when you encounter things that remind you of your loss.[3] Not all women will have these particular responses but anxiety is one normal response to an extremely stressful event. If this is something you struggle with, understand that while the pregnancy loss probably will continue to be a source of anxiety, the symptoms should begin diminishing within six months.

Depression

We tend to use the word "depression" loosely, meaning any one of a number of negative emotional states. But clinical depression, as we talked about in chapter 3, is something different and specific. Studies have found that women who have recently had miscarriages are at an elevated risk for experiencing symptoms of depression.[4] It seems that women who are more likely to experience depression fall into one of the following categories:

> They believe their miscarriage was personally significant.
> They don't have a good community of support.
> They don't have as much emotional strength. (If you already struggle with depression, for example, you are at greater risk of suffering from a depressive response after your loss.)
> They use passive coping strategies. (Examples of these would be keeping to yourself, wishing it would all go away, or blaming yourself for the loss.)
> They have lower incomes. (Why this is so is unclear, but may be because private doctors' offices provide more emotional support to patients, or because lower-income families often have less free time to continue to provide social support over weeks and months.)
> They do not get pregnant or have a baby within a year of their loss.[5]

If you are struggling with depression after your miscarriage, you may find that you cannot function normally, either because you seem to be walking around in a fog or because you can't stop thinking about the miscarriage. You may not be able to keep from crying. You may have trouble sleeping or sleep too much. You may not be able to enjoy things you previously liked doing. You may eat too much or not enough. You may have trouble finding the motivation to do much of anything. It is hard to see depression when you're experiencing it yourself because you tend to see everything through a depressed filter. Comments that would not bother you in a nondepressed state come across as incredibly hurtful. Unrelated events or words somehow tie back to your loss. And you often don't realize that you're not reacting or responding as you would if you were not depressed.

Many people experience seasons of situational depression, especially after significant losses. Your depression should ease in that six-month period. If your loved ones express concern about your emotional state, listen to them and seek support processing your loss and caring for yourself.

Grief

This may seem like a no-brainer, but it can help to look at the symptoms of normal grief for some reassurance that your feelings are normal, not an over-reaction. One team of psychologists categorizes the descriptors of grief four ways: affectively (how you feel), behaviorally (how you act), cognitively (how you think), and physiologically (how your body responds). They say that grief usually shows up in the following ways:

> Affectively, people are depressed, despairing, dejected, angry, and hostile. Behaviorally, they tend to act agitated and fatigued, cry spontaneously, and are socially withdrawn. Cognitively, they are preoccupied with thoughts of the deceased, have negative self-judgments, feel hopeless and helpless, have a sense of unreality, and experience memory and concentration problems. Physiologically, there is a loss of appetite, sleep disturbance, energy loss and exhaustion, somatic complaints, and physical complaints often similar to what the deceased endured. Yearning, or a deep longing for the deceased, has been identified in a recent study as the most salient element of grief among 233 individuals who were administered the Inventory of Complicated Grief-Revised scale.[6]

Do any of these sound familiar? If so, you are not alone. A majority of women seem to experience a grief reaction following a miscarriage. One study found that women described those feelings of grief in the following way:

> Initially, a sense of shock and unreality is described, followed by feelings of confusion over the sudden disappearance of a maternal role, and disappointment over the loss of an anticipated future. The intensity of grief is described as similar to the intensity of grief individuals experience after other types of significant losses, such as that of a family member. Also described are symptoms of stress, sadness, depression, guilt, and self-blame.[7]

Again, these are normal feelings, shared by many women. And they will usually diminish significantly after the first six months.

The first six months tend to be marked by strong emotional responses. You will discover that these responses can be triggered by things that seem related as well as things that don't. Going to the home improvement store can make you think about the shopping trip when you were shopping for lightbulbs but spent thirty minutes looking at paint chips for the nursery. Your eyes may be drawn inexorably to the displays of baby food and bottles in the grocery store, and taking a walk can make you think of the walks you planned to take with baby. Many women find that their community suddenly seems full of pregnant women or women with small babies. Christine said that her grief showed up "every time I saw a baby; each year on my due date; seeing other people have babies (who did *not* want a baby and would neglect or abuse them)." Many women have vivid nightmares. When your pain is so close to the surface, it does not take much to trigger it. The hopeful news is that your pain should lessen gradually and will eventually get easier to bear.

ANNIVERSARIES AND LATER MILESTONES

After any kind of loss, grief can resurface in surprising ways. Months after they believed they had successfully moved through their pain, some women told me, they would experience a resurgence of more intense grief or suddenly become agitated or anxious with no apparent cause. Then they would look at a calendar or talk to a friend and realize that it was the baby's projected due date or the first anniversary of the loss. Other women have found that if friends had children close to when they had expected to have a baby, the milestones reached by those living children could cause grief to surface again. One woman told me that she and her sister had been pregnant at the same time. She miscarried, and her sister delivered a healthy child. Despite the pain and disappointment involved for both of them, their relationship continued to thrive. However, the woman who had lost her pregnancy found her nephew's first couple of birthday parties and holidays almost unbearable because they would remind her so strongly of the cousin who had been expected to be part of those celebrations. Grief can jump out and surprise you during times of later trauma as well. Debbie shared, "It was several years after both children were born, and I was going through a difficult time in my life, that all the emotions from the miscarriages that I had pushed aside came rushing back."

Holidays and other special occasions can also trigger renewed grief. Parents often vividly imagine the child they will have participating in their family traditions—sitting in the heirloom high chair on Thanksgiving, going with the family to midnight Easter Vigil services, holding the Baby Jesus figurine as the Christmas story is told on Christmas Eve—and when those traditions take place without the child there, the loss can seem fresh again. A family shared with me that it was almost a year before they would go to church on Sundays when they knew a baby was being baptized. They had looked forward so strongly to their own child's baptism that watching the sacrament that would never be administered to their own baby was too pain-ful for them.

Grief continues to resurface for some people years and years later. The year the baby would have reached a milestone—sixteen, for example, or high school graduation—can be a difficult one. For many parents of other children, when their living children reach various milestones, even through the celebration there continues to be a nagging sense of someone missing from the family unit. For most people, these later grief responses are qui-eter, much less intense. For some people, however, especially people who have not had the opportunity or the support to fully grieve the loss in the first place, the resurfacing of the grief can be incredibly intense and painful, even years later. If this happens to you, I encourage you to find a competent, sensitive counselor who can help you discover why your grief remains so concentrated.

LATER PREGNANCIES

Fast-forward to six weeks or six months after your miscarriage, when you have decided you're ready and your doctor has given you and your partner clearance to start trying again. Many women find both the process of trying to become pregnant after a miscarriage and any subsequent pregnancies to be fraught with fear and anxiety. The entire process seems tinged with grief. Many women and men hesitate to get too invested in subsequent pregnan-cies because they do not want to go through the same intensity of grief they experienced with the miscarriage. Megan shared:

> [Miscarriage] robs you of the excitement of getting pregnant the next time. When we got pregnant the third time it was so totally anticlimac-tic. I took a test, I told Brad I was pregnant, and he said OK. I'm not sure we even talked about it for a week. And then we spent the next two months trying to avoid thinking about being pregnant. I was filling out a baby book recently, and it asked when I found out I was pregnant and had room for the whole story. I didn't remember the date and there was no story. I realized my miscarriages had robbed Isaac of that story. Will he ask someday why I wasn't excited when I found out I was pregnant with him?

This complicated process of trying to become pregnant again after miscar-riage can be another stressor on already-fragile marriages and relationships. JoAnn shared, "Throughout this time [of my subsequent pregnancy] I was constantly nervous, worried, and basically filled with anxiety. My former husband had little patience with me, and entered into the first of many extramarital affairs, which ultimately destroyed our marriage several years later."

Some women get pregnant right away and spend the rest of their pregnancy on the nursing hotline, checking out strange twinges and symptoms, watching for the ominous spotting, sure that something is going to go wrong. Other women enter that limbo of trying to become pregnant, the cyclical process of waiting, waiting, timing sex perfectly, waiting, waiting, and then watching the hopes for that cycle's conception bleed away once again. For some women, the monthly period can bring back recurring grief related to their miscarriage. And some women begin a long struggle with secondary infertility.

Molly found, however, that God used even that complicated journey through postmiscarriage pregnancy to nurture her and her husband:

> We tried after this [second] miscarriage for what seemed like an eternity to get pregnant again. It had happened so easily before, so when it didn't happen right away, I started to become a crazy woman! Sex with my husband was not at all fun during this time, and I was quite the militant about when, what time, and how often we were going to do it to make a baby. My husband felt pressured and robotic. This went on for about eight months, and then we realized that it is all God's plan of when and *if* this will happen. We decided to take the pressure off, realize that maybe we are a family trio, perhaps consider adoption down the road, and ease up on the mechanical sex, laugh at ourselves, etc. No kidding, the next month we became pregnant! We were so relieved, but there was that nervousness again. For whatever reason in my bathroom one morning (these things hit you in the oddest places), I realized that God did not want me to worry. What will happen will happen. I got on my knees then and there and just gave the worry all up to God. I did pray for a healthy baby, of course, but I also prayed for his help with whatever may happen. I didn't want to go through an entire pregnancy full of stress. I realized another important lesson: constantly worrying about miscarriage during pregnancy takes away from the miracle inside you that God has created. Worry takes away the joy and excitement of this gift. What a difference this made in my pregnancy. I really felt God's presence during this time.

You may or may not be able to see God at work in your experience as Molly did. But for some women, even through the difficult journey of postmiscarriage pregnancy, God can be sensed at work, leading and loving them even through the wilderness months.

PART OF YOUR STORY . . .

This leads us into a delicate conversation. In the very painful months directly following your loss, I might even recommend that you *not* read this part of the book, that you skip it and come back to it some months later. But I include this portion because despite the pain, the grief, the magnitude of the loss of a miscarriage, many women eventually find ways to incorporate that loss into their life stories. Loss and grief and tragedy are knit in to the story of God's people, after all. It was in the endless years of exile—hungry, homeless, and increasingly hopeless—that the Israelites came to know God's providence and steadfast love in a new and powerful way. It was in the season of grief over the loss of her first husband, the season of being a foreigner in a strange land and not having enough to eat, that Ruth discovered God's providence through Boaz's generosity and her own courage. It is often when everything else is stripped away that we can see and sense God's presence and care most clearly.

Faithful Christians understand God's providence in different ways, and, as we discussed in chapter 5, it is not always possible for us to pin down God's will. However, whether you understand your loss as being *willed* by God or as being *allowed* by God, we know that the God of Jesus Christ can work within and through that loss to bring redemption and healing to you and to others. What do I mean by that? I would say that God *allowed* my losses to happen. And God took those very losses, full of pain and sorrow and disappointment, and has wrapped them up into God's ongoing work of bringing new life to a broken world. Through that experience, my understanding of God's loving heartbreak over the state of the world has deepened. Through that experience, I have found that my ability to care for others in their own grief has been broadened. Through that experience, I have learned important things about the fragility of life, the inevitability of death, and the essential importance of following a God who promises us that absolutely nothing can separate us from the divine Life, divine Love. Through that experience, I have learned that I can trust and rely on my husband through whatever our marriage brings. Because of those other losses, my two daughters, unique and irreplaceable and beloved persons in their own right, exist.

Is that why I had miscarriages? I don't believe so. This is not a system of exchanges, in which those good things were bought at the price of my unborn babies' lives. But *are* these good things, things of God, that have grown out of the soil broken by my losses? Yes, they are. And in my life, they testify to a God who loves the world enough to use broken things to make life whole, the God who used the tragedy of the cross, the tragedy of the broken life and heart of God, to bring a sullen, sinning world back into the God-life again.

Other women have testified to the ways in which they have seen God at work through their own losses. LeAnn said:

> I feel these experiences have left me more sensitive to others around me. I know that I will never have the right words to say to someone that is grieving any loss, but rather I try to let them know they can call on me for help or to listen. Although society may not agree, I feel that the grief that I have experienced through miscarriage is similar to many other types of grief. I feel this has given me empathy for others. The first experience of miscarriage did "make sense" in my life after the birth of my son, but the second experience left a hole in my heart that has not yet been filled.

"I believe [God] is building my character," said Tammy, "and I am learning to trust him more." Heather shared, "[God] has given me two beautiful children, and he has deepened my relationship with him. I also have an awareness of the pain that those who miscarry go through." JoAnn said:

> Sadly my marriage ended in June of 1976, but God, in his wisdom and mercy, gave me the strength and the guidance I had prayed for long ago. I survived, with his help, became born again in September of 1988, and continue to be blessed beyond measure. That young, naive girl no longer exists, but in her place is a 65-year-old woman who has learned to put all her trust in the Lord. He will do all things in his time, and according to his will, because he loves each of us . . . his precious children.

And Susan narrated her experience this way:

> I just got back from a trip with Jack [my son] to visit my parents and saw one of my best friends. She asked if I ever think about the baby that we lost. I answered her truthfully: Yes, I still think about it—in terms of how old it would be now, what it would be doing—but immediately I think about Jack. If I had the baby from my first pregnancy, we would never have had Jack. I think that's where God fits into all of this for me: we have the child we were meant to have. We are so lucky.

You may not be ready for this conversation right now. That is fine. You should not feel as if you ought to find a reason that your miscarriage happened; you should not feel as if you ought to be able to see God's hand at work through the loss. But the loss becomes part of your own story, an important chapter in your own journey with those you love, your own journey with God. And God can and will bring new life out of death, joy out of mourning, resurrection out of crucifixion . . . one day.

REFLECTION QUESTIONS

1. What aspects of your grief have surprised you?
2. Are there ways you have seen God at work through or despite your experience of pregnancy loss?

EXERCISE

Think about a date that has meaning for you as it relates to your pregnancy loss. It could be the date you found out you were pregnant, the date of the miscarriage, the date you shared the news of your pregnancy with the family, the projected due date, or another date. With your partner or alone, plan a way to memorialize that date the next time it comes around. (You can find some ideas about how to do this in chapters 13 and 14.) Mark your calendar.

Chapter 13

How to Say Good-Bye

*R*eturn with me to that CPE session in which I realized how much my miscarriage was still hurting me. After the silence had stretched on and I'd gone through a good chunk of the ubiquitous hospital box of tissues, Timothy, one of my peers, cleared his throat. I immediately dreaded what he was going to say. Timothy was doing his second unit of CPE and tended toward ruthlessly incisive and relentless probing into sensitive parts of our psyches. He leaned forward into the circle and said, "We've realized this summer that you don't do a good job of letting other people care for you."

I nodded silently, my eyes still on the wad of scratchy tissues in my lap.

"Well," he said gently, "would you let us minister to you?"

I looked at him then, confused.

"Would you let us plan and hold a memorial service for your baby?"

My tears started to well up again. The response trying to push its way out of my mouth went something like, "Oh, no, thank you so much, but it's really not necessary; I don't want to be a hassle, and you all have so much going on." But getting in the way of my tongue was the fact that he had said, "your baby." I had been unable to care for that baby, and she deserved to have someone do something for her. (My husband might have suggested that I did, too.) So, feeling awkward, but carefully practicing "letting other people care for me," I said, "All right. Yes, I would like that." My peers and supervisor then dismissed me from the room so they could do the planning.

I was incredibly uncomfortable about the whole thing, frankly. I didn't want to be the center of attention; I still suspected that I was overreacting to the miscarriage and was worried that this service would feel like an elaborate farce, my peers' way of humoring me. But they were already planning things, and it was too late to turn back.

The service was hosted at the church Timothy was serving. We pulled into the dusty parking lot of a small African Methodist Episcopal church snugged into the tree line off a curvy road not far from the hospital. Feeling conspicuous in my nice clothes on a weekday morning, I held Chris's hand as we entered the coolness of the sanctuary and smelled the beautiful, musty, old-church smell. The altar was lit with candles. Along with Chris and me, his sister and brother-in-law and parents were there; all of our South Carolina immediate family attended together. We chose places in a pew on the right-hand side. Besides our little group, a few of the other CPE supervisors and peers sat scattered in the other pews.

Timothy and my supervisor, Robert, presided, resplendent in their full, black vestments, gold-embroidered stoles hanging down over velvety, crimson-corded lapels. We prayed and read Scripture, responded in the words of a liturgy. My awkwardness began to melt away as I felt more and more strongly how appropriate this was.

Another of my peers, a Presbyterian pastor named Meghan who was close to my own age and also from the Midwest, had been elected to preach. She looked lovingly at me during the sermon,[1] which fell like balm on my wounds, soft and gentle, until the moment when I heard God's voice echo in Meghan's. As she leaned forward, she said, "Elise, I have heard you speak of your child who was lost . . . but here is the truth: *What is found in God is never lost. What is found in God is never, ever truly lost.*" The Holy Spirit gripped me, carving those words into me, giving me the reassurance I had longed for, searing it into my heart and my mind. *What is found in Me is never, ever lost.* The word I had been waiting for, the word I had been searching for, asking for, had finally come. The details didn't have to be clear; God had given me hope and assurance that somehow, in some way, God would take care of my unborn baby. God *would*. My little one was not lost, not abandoned, not wandering through the cosmos or suspended in a state of nonbeing. My lost unborn baby was with God.

We shared Communion that day, and I wept as I sensed the cords that bound together the family of God, the communion of saints over time, over place, pulled across every division to be part of the meal laid by Jesus, the body and blood that incorporated all of us, the "living, the unborn, the dead." I knew that the same wounded hands that served me cradled the life that had been lost from my body, but not lost from the body of Christ. I whispered, "Thanks be to God. Thanks be to Christ," as the bread and juice tingled on my lips.

Did this experience cause my grief to magically, miraculously disappear? By no means. I continued to have times of sadness, times of self-blame. I continued to miss my baby. I continued to have fears and anxiety about getting pregnant again, concerns about our family's future. I continued to experience grief and envy when I spent time with other people who had children, continued to be sad on the anniversaries connected to our loss. I even continued to search for answers—in fact, one of the first things I did when I got back to school that next semester was to find a professor who would supervise an independent study on pregnancy loss. But all the same, something important happened in that service of worship. I went from feeling alone in my loss (despite the presence of so many supportive people in my life) to feeling as though I had stepped back into the community of faith and had found within it a story that was big enough and rich enough to hold me, even as I suffered. The body of Christ, the few representatives of it who were there, had said, "Yes, you have a right to mourn. This loss should affect you. It affects us as well. We mourn with you. We bring you and your unborn child before God. We proclaim the truth about God's love for God's world, about God's entry into our own suffering. And together we reach out for the hope that one day God will finally right what is wrong, that one day redemption will be accomplished and our mourning will be turned to dancing."

Why do concrete practices such as services of worship, memorial acts, and choosing tokens of remembrance matter so much and can have such a profound healing effect on our grief?

First, concrete practices *reflect the reality of our loss.* Especially with miscarriage, we lack both a cultural and a personal assurance that there is, in fact, a reason for our grief. I and many others have felt the discrepancy between our own feelings of pain and the dismissive ways that our culture responds to that pain. It's easy to wonder if you're overreacting, making a big deal out of nothing, because no one else seems to think this should matter very much. Concrete practices, rituals and acts, reassure us that our loss was real, that our grief is founded in a true event, that others recognize the source of our pain, that we're not imagining the whole thing.

Second, concrete practices *give us and others memories of the life we've lost.* The only direct memories of that life that we are likely to have will fall into two categories: "interior" memories of the ways in which the mother's body was affected physically (and therefore that are not shared by anyone else; even if you told your husband about your morning sickness, he was not constantly leaving departmental meetings to retch into the toilet) and memories of the miscarriage event. Some people may have an ultrasound image or a memory of hearing the baby's heart beat as well. One of the ways human beings process grief and loss is by replaying, over and over again, memories of the deceased. This is at least partially the function of the traditional wake, during which family members and friends and neighbors share stories about the life of the person who has died, wrapping up their common memory of that life as it touched the lives of the community, testifying to the difference that life made in their own lives, understanding the difference it will make to have that life absent. With a miscarriage, however, women are likely to replay over and over again both the feelings of the pregnancy (which no one else can share or contribute their own memories to) and their experience of the loss, which may be quite traumatic. Concrete practices create cords of common memory that can bind the bereaved mother with her spouse and with others who share in memory making with her. And they give those who are grieving this loss new memories connected to the life that has died, new memories to replay as they come to terms with their loss.

Finally, concrete practices *give us an opportunity to turn things over to God*, formally, directly, as well as to *receive testimony to hope and to God's love*. A ritual act or act of worship can offer us a moment in time that is set apart for the sacred task of memorializing the life of the unborn child in the presence of God. It can give us a chance to say, "God, I do not understand what all this means, but I offer the life of this child and my life from this moment on to you." And it sets aside sacred time to hear God's response, in the words of Scripture and in the words of the community. In some ways, this is similar to what we do in weddings or baptisms or funerals. In all three of these cases, what is being marked is an enormous life transition, a transition that no worship service, no memorial act, can fully encompass. But in all three cases, the community of God gathers to commit together to a new way forward. The community of God comes together to say, "From now on, we will live *this* way." From now on, we will be faithful to one another in marriage (even though we don't have a clue what that will look like ten years down the road) and we trust that if you are with us, Lord, we will be enabled to be faithful. From now on, we will bring up this child in your household (even though we don't know what that will mean when she is ten or twenty or sixty) and we trust that if you are with us, Lord, she will be your daughter all her days. From now on, we will commit the life of this one we loved to you (even though we no longer see him) and we trust that if you are with us, Lord, he will be ushered into your kingdom. The married couple continues to learn how to negotiate conflict and transition, the baptized child continues to walk along paths that look faithful some days and not other days, the bereaved widow continues to hold her husband's wedding band and cry herself to sleep. Something has changed, nevertheless. The path ahead is marked, and its ending point is found in the security of the steadfast love of God. And we are reminded, assured, of God's presence with us, even when we may not be able to feel it.

MEMORIAL ACTS

So what kinds of concrete practices are there? What do people do? One category of practices could be called memorial acts, which you might do alone or with family or friends to memorialize your baby.

The first and perhaps most important of these acts is to name your child. How you do this will be very personal. Some people know the gender of their unborn baby; others don't. Some women have an intuition about gender; if you think your baby was a girl or a boy, name the child appropriately. Others don't have an intuition, and they may name their child something gender-neutral. Lots of couples choose to give the child a name that has special meaning, perhaps finding an appropriate name in their family history, in a Bible story, or in the history of a saint.

After naming the child, reflecting the reality of that beloved individual's presence in the life of their family and of the people of God, some people choose to do something concrete in the lost child's name, something that will honor the child's memory by making a contribution to a good cause. Some possibilities:

> Plant a tree or other special plant. (You could add a small plaque on the ground or eventually hang a special birdhouse or set of wind chimes in the tree. Some trees, rosebushes, and other perennial plants have names you might find symbolic.)
>
> Give money to an appropriate organization. (The options are endless. Possibilities include organizations the parents are already committed to, such as their own church or local school; organizations like the March of Dimes that focus on infants who are born too early; organizations that care for children, such as orphanages, child crisis centers, or child support programs; and organizations whose mission has some connection to the unborn child's death date or projected due date.)
>
> Give money to a particular child. (Some families have chosen to support a child through World Vision or a similar organization. You could also choose to pay for a child's cleft palate surgery or other need in memory of your own unborn child. Your pastor or missions team may know of a local child with needs you could help to meet.)
>
> Sponsor an animal. (Many zoos and other organizations offer naming opportunities or chances to share in providing care for an animal for a certain length of time.)
>
> Contribute to your hospital's neonatal intensive care unit in your unborn child's memory.
>
> Work with a local charitable organization to provide diapers and formula for local needy mothers.

Ask whether your local hospital or doctor's office would let you provide (or contribute toward an existing program to provide) some sort of gift for other families who lose pregnancies (a baby memento, a keepsake Bible, a book, a prayer on a card).

People sometimes find it meaningful to choose one or more items to keep in memory of their child. These memory items could be absolutely anything. What matters is that you (and your partner) select something that is special to you and reminds you of your child. Ideas might include:

A keepsake jewelry item (Artists can produce customized pieces for you; options might include a bracelet with name or date engraved on it, a birthstone ring, or a special necklace.)

A memorial plaque (You could engrave a Scripture passage or simply your child's name and the date of your miscarriage. This could be placed in your own garden, but you could also ask your pastor if your church has a memorial garden, columbarium area, or other place where it might be appropriate to place something small. Some churches might have opportunities to place a piece of sculpture or furniture in a garden or room in memory of your unborn child, but most churches have careful policies about grounds and buildings, so you will need to talk to your pastor before making any plans or setting your heart on a particular idea.)

A memory box (You could create or purchase a special box or just use a shoebox to hold ultrasound images, cards or dried flowers you received, records of your hospital or doctor visit(s), a baby book if you already started one for this child, copies of prayers or worship service bulletins, maternity clothing, the pregnancy test, baby clothes, or any other items you find meaningful.)

A candle to light on anniversaries (A short service to support a candle-lighting practice is in chapter 14.)

A natural item (Perhaps a certain flower was in bloom when you first became pregnant or when you lost the baby, or you might dry and keep a leaf from a tree outside the nursery window. Anything you associate with your lost baby or with God's presence during your grief would be appropriate.)

Something you (and your partner) shop for and select for the purpose (perhaps a special piece of artwork, a book of poetry, a musical instrument, or a Christmas tree ornament)

Something you (or your partner) create (If you draw or paint or sculpt, if you do needlework or knitting, if you garden or do woodworking, if you write poetry, essays, or music—any of these and more can give you an opportunity to create something special as a memorial piece.)

You may be able to think of another kind of memorial act you could do that would give you comfort. If you do choose to do something, please remember this: these acts are not magical. They will not immediately heal your pain; they will not bring your baby back again. But just like a carefully preserved lock of hair in another era, these memorial acts and items can provide you with a tangible connection to the effect your lost child had on your own life. They can provide you with an opportunity to mourn what you lost, to remember how your loss changed you, and, perhaps in time, to celebrate the gift that child was to you, even for the weeks or months you were together. They can provide you with a channel to receive God's grace. And especially if you perform acts of generosity in memory of your child, you will be able to see a specific, concrete good that was inspired by your little one's short but meaningful life.

WORSHIP ACTS

Some people are very uncomfortable with the idea of a worship service but they can be healing. We celebrate and mourn most of life's pivotal moments purposefully in the presence of God; it is appropriate to mourn this crucial loss in God's presence as well. That said, it is not necessary to be in a church building to be in the presence of God. Below is a list of different ideas and ways to commit an unborn child to God through acts of worship. Examples of all of these different types of services are found in chapter 14.

A SERVICE IN THE CHURCH

All of these church services would need to be planned with your pastor, and some of them would need to involve church members and staff members who participate in worship planning. You should schedule a time to meet with the pastor to talk about what options might be available and appropriate for your community of faith. You could also ask your partner, a family member, or a close friend to do this. Don't be afraid to state clearly what you believe would be most healing for you.

A Service That Takes Place as Part of the Regular Sunday Morning Service

You may or may not feel comfortable with this, but for some people and some faith communities, it makes sense to have this kind of service incorporated into regular weekly worship. Your pastor and church will have to be comfortable with this as well. If this is the route you and your pastor find appropriate, the service, similar to the baptismal service, would probably consist of a relatively short liturgy, perhaps with a special song or hymn sung. All Saints' Sunday at the beginning of November may be a time your pastor would choose to incorporate such a memorial service.

A Special Service Designed for All Women in the Church or Community Who Have Had Miscarriages

Again, planning and executing this kind of service would be up to your pastor or a group within your church. This service would probably be similar to a memorial service in your tradition.

A Private Service for You and Whomever You Invite

I have held these services for women and immediate family members and close friends and for just the grieving couple. It could be structured like a funeral or like a short healing service. Opening such a service to members of the church who want to attend can be a surprising source of support and love, but it is not necessary.

A SERVICE IN YOUR HOME

The tradition of worshiping in the home as a family or with small groups of close brothers and sisters in Christ is as old as the church. This kind of service, usually less formal than a service in a church, can be healing for a family unit if all members agree to participate. It can provide a safe place to continue processing with older children, or for husbands and wives to care for each other, conscious of God's presence with them in a sacred moment. While you can certainly invite your pastor to come to your home to lead such a service, you may also choose to lead it yourselves. Concrete acts such as washing one another's feet, anointing one another with oil, or establishing a memorial item as part of the worship (planting a tree, for example, writing prayers for your child's memory box, or writing a family letter to the child you are going to sponsor) can all be powerful and appropriate ways to turn to God together.

A WORSHIP PILGRIMAGE

A pilgrim is a traveler on the way to a sacred place, on the way to find the holy. Your worship service could take place as part of a pilgrimage as well. You could hold a worship service in a place that has meaning for you or your family. You could even take a trip to a state park or mountain retreat and plan worship for that location. Some denominations own campgrounds, and often the directors of those campgrounds are pastors themselves, or persons who could help you think through how you might carry out a pilgrimage at their particular site. Using the special features of natural sites (rivers, lakes, dunes, beaches, pine groves, mountains) can be a special and symbolic way to mark your own worship pilgrimage.

No matter what path you choose, no matter what acts of worship, memorials, or other ways you decide it is appropriate for you to respond, please do choose at least one way for you and your family to formally say good-bye and remember your lost child. Your child's life mattered, both to you and to God. It is right to find ways to mark and recognize the significance of that loss in your own journey.

The part of the journey I am taking with you draws to a close here, but your own journey continues. I pray that as you walk along this road that is so often marked with grief, you will find yourself led eventually through this valley and into an easier place. I pray as well that you will allow this cup of suffering to change you, to deepen you, to strengthen, in the end, your relationships with those you love, and most of all, with the God who loves you, even in the dark times. May God accompany you and bless you, and may God give you what you need both to drink this bitter cup to the full and then to emerge again into the sunshine—changed, yes, but rooted even more deeply in the unfailing heart of the Divine, the One apart from whom a sparrow does not fall, the One who holds your lost little ones as well.

REFLECTION QUESTIONS

1. Which of the options for memorial acts is most appealing to you? Why?
2. Which of the options for worship practices is most appealing to you? Why?

EXERCISE

If you have not already, with your partner or alone, make plans to concretely, formally say good-bye to your child, either through a service of worship or through a memorial act. (It is not necessary to use one of the options laid out in this chapter.) What planning, if any, needs to take place? Line up the help you will need to make it happen.

Chapter 14

Resources and Getting Help

BOOKS

Some other books have been written on miscarriage that you may find helpful. Many of the published works cover infertility, stillbirth, and neonatal or infant death as well as miscarriage. When you are grieving following a miscarriage, it is easy to look at one of these books and feel guilty, as if your grief doesn't compare to the grief of a parent who has lost a born infant. This is why I don't believe that these topics are best treated together. Losses should not be compared. You would never walk up to a person who was grieving the loss of a beloved adult sibling and say, "You shouldn't be hurting, because there are people in Darfur who are tortured to death, and your loss isn't as bad as that." That is nonsense. Different losses have different characteristics, and your grief over your miscarriage may, in fact, be both different and less traumatic than the grief of a parent who loses a three-month-old infant to SIDS or a three-year-old child to leukemia. But just as losing a spouse in old age to cancer may be "better" than losing him to suicide in his thirties, you would never expect to avoid grief over the later loss. Your grief is reasonable and normal. Do not feel guilty because your loss wasn't "worse"; don't compare it to other losses.

I am going to recommend a few books; if you want to read further, check your library or do an online search (paying attention to the posted reviews from other readers).

General Resources

Ingrid Kohn and Perry-Lynn Moffitt, *A Silent Sorrow: Pregnancy Loss; Guidance and Support for You and Your Family* (New York: Routledge,

2000). One of the most comprehensive resources available and now in its second edition, *A Silent Sorrow* provides an extensive and detailed overview of pregnancy loss, including medical, emotional, and relational treatments of the topic. Although it has specific sections devoted to losses at different gestational ages, the book as a whole is intended to cover any type of pregnancy loss, from early miscarriage to stillbirth. It is densely written, although readable.

Kim Kluger-Bell, *Unspeakable Losses: Healing from Miscarriage, Abortion, and Other Pregnancy Loss* (New York: W. W. Norton, 1998). Sensitively written by a psychotherapist who experienced miscarriage herself, this book has the benefit of focusing on pregnancy loss rather than infant death. Its psychological subtext is rich, and it may be useful as you explore both the ways in which your pregnancy loss is interpreted through your own life circumstances and history and the ways in which it affects your worldview into the future.

Medical Resources

Bruce Young and Amy Zavatto, *Miscarriage, Medicine, and Miracles: Everything You Need to Know about Miscarriage* (New York: Bantam Dell, 2008). This is one of the best medical resources available to laypeople. It is the most recently published (as of this writing) and contains lots of readable medical details. If you crave biological reasons for your miscarriage or you would like to have an informed conversation with your doctor, I recommend reading this book as an alternative to Web searches, which may or may not turn up good information and will almost certainly overwhelm you with inessential details. Let this (or one of the following books) be your primary medical source, and allow your doctor to help you interpret the information you glean from it. Despite its ambitious subtitle, the book does not, however, contain "everything" a person may need to know about miscarriage; the section on "understanding" (including "grieving, coping, hoping") is just six pages out of the book's 334. Cowritten by a specialist physician and a freelance writer, it is accessible and a fairly easy read.

Jon Cohen, *Coming to Term: Uncovering the Truth about Miscarriage* (New York: Houghton Mifflin, 2005). Jon Cohen is a journalist who is experienced in translating medical research into language that laypeople can understand. After his wife suffered repeated miscarriages, he researched pregnancy loss and wrote this highly readable, information-stuffed account of the medical side of miscarriage.

Henry M. Lerner, *Miscarriage: Why It Happens and How Best to Reduce Your Risks* (Cambridge: Perseus Publishing, 2003). Written by an ob-gyn, this book reads like a layperson's introductory diagnostic medical text. It is fairly thorough and detailed, and many readers will appreciate the detailed explanation of reproductive cycles and the diagrams of reproductive anatomy. Lerner goes through several causes of miscarriage and explains diagnosis and treatment for each.

Story-Sharing Resources

Marie Allen and Shelly Marks, *Miscarriage: Women Sharing from the Heart* (New York: John Wiley & Sons, 1993). This book takes a different approach to miscarriage, walking the reader through the experience using almost entirely quotes from one hundred women who were interviewed for the purpose. I like two things about this book: first, that it focuses exclusively on miscarriage; and second, that it offers companionship through the real voices of diverse women who have been affected by miscarriage.

Rachel Faldet and Karen Fitton, eds., *Our Stories of Miscarriage: Healing with Words* (Minneapolis: Fairview Press, 1997). This compilation of short stories, poems, and other creative reflections on miscarriage includes stories from both women and men and is bittersweet, poignant, and lovely. I found this in a public library not long after our own first loss, and I remember reading it cover to cover, tears streaming down my cheeks. It's a wonderful testimony that those who are grieving do not walk the road alone.

Jessica Berger Gross, ed., *About What Was Lost: Twenty Writers on Miscarriage, Healing, and Hope* (London: Penguin Books, 2007). As you might imagine, this anthology is exceedingly well-written, an artistic montage that can help you find yourself in the portrayals of the loss.

Christian/Inspirational Resources

Jenny Schroedel, *Naming the Child: Hope-Filled Reflections on Miscarriage, Stillbirth, and Infant Death* (Brewster, MA: Paraclete Press, 2009). In one way, I loved this book, because it shared so many stories, it is beautifully written, and it is one of the few deeply imagined Christian resources available. However, it does spend a great deal of time on stillbirth and infant death. You may want to look at the author's Web site before purchasing the book. The site is lovely and includes interactive features: www.namingthechild.com.

Nadine Pence Frantz and Mary T. Stimming, eds., *Hope Deferred: Heart-Healing Reflections on Reproductive Loss* (Cleveland: Pilgrim Press, 2005). This is the first and currently only available collection of theological essays about reproductive loss, including infertility and miscarriage. It may not be what many women are looking for in the immediate aftermath of their loss, but it is a valuable contribution for those who are interested in theologically thinking through what God has to say about these particular losses.

ONLINE RESOURCES

If you do some online research into miscarriage, make sure that you're looking at Web sites that provide trustworthy information. As interesting and sometimes gratifying as it can be to pore over postings from random women and men across the globe, the collections of reasons, symptoms, and reported conversations with medical providers offered on many sites are not an accurate source of information. Some established Web sites that have reliable information include the following:

www.marchofdimes.com. The March of Dimes calls itself the "leading nonprofit organization for pregnancy and baby health." Its site has basic medical information about miscarriage as well as ectopic and molar pregnancies.

www.nationalshare.org. The mission of Share, according to its Web site, is to "serve those whose lives are touched by the tragic death of a baby through early pregnancy loss, stillbirth, or in the first few months of life." This is quite a comprehensive site, offering online support groups and medical information as well as a request form for a free support packet containing emotional-support resources and information about local support groups.

http://pregnancyloss.info. Of all the sites started and maintained by individuals, this one is the best. It is comprehensive in topic and offers several ways to connect with other bereaved folks. It also contains an extensive FAQ section full of most of the questions you will want to have addressed.

SUPPORT COMMUNITIES

National Share, an organization providing support and advocacy for those who have experienced pregnancy or early infant loss, has a list

of local support groups on its Web site, http://www.nationalshare
.org/Groups.html. Most states have at least one group available.

The best local information about support groups will almost certainly
be available through your local hospital or doctor's or midwife's
office.

If there are no local support groups available, it is possible for you to
start one. Talk to your doctor or midwife to see how you might go
about this. You can also find limited but helpful support online.

PRAYERS

A Prayer during Miscarriage

God of all creation, we don't know what to say.
We can't believe this is happening to us, to the baby we love.
We don't know how to feel.
We don't know what to say.
We are angry, grief-stricken, bewildered, and hurt.
Let us feel your presence in these painful hours.
Surround us with a sense of your steadfast love.
Give the medical staff who will care for us compassion and wisdom.
Help us know where to find support.
Care for our baby, now that we cannot.
Gather up our lives and the precious life that is ending, and hold us
    close.
In the name of Jesus, who walks through heartbreak with us, Amen.

A Prayer over the Child's Body

Merciful God, all that you give us is yours.
We give you thanks for the time we have known and loved this little one.
We grieve that our time together is over so soon.
We have given *him/her* the name of _____.
"Whether we live, or whether we die, we are the Lord's," and so we give
    Name back to you, knowing that *his/her* life is safe in your keeping.
Bless *him/her* in the life to come.
Give *him/her* unending knowledge of your steadfast love and outpoured
    grace.
Allow all of us to stand before you one day,
    no longer seeing dimly through a clouded glass,
    but finally seeing face to face.
In the name of Jesus the Christ we pray. Amen.

A Prayer for Healing

It can be powerful to accompany a prayer for healing with actions: kneeling together and placing your hands on the person for whom you are praying, using scented oil to anoint the person in need of healing; praying standing with arms outstretched, and so on. The prayer below can be reworded so that a spouse, friend, or pastor could pray it on behalf of a hurting woman or couple.

> Jesus, during your time on earth, you healed broken people who came to you.
> I come to you now seeking healing for my own brokenness.
> My body feels broken.
> My spirit seems broken.
> My heart is broken.
> Please, lay your hands on my life:
>   make me physically whole again;
>   help me trust you in this shadow season;
>   fill the excruciating hole in my heart.
> Nurture and restore the relationships that sustain me:
>   my relationship with my spouse;
>   my relationship with my own parents;
>   my relationships with my friends;
>   my relationship with you.
> Hold me during this night,
>   so I can be watching when the morning breaks and joy comes again.
> In your name, Amen.

MEMORIAL WORSHIP SERVICES (COMPLETE)

A Service of Hope after Loss of Pregnancy

This service was written by a theologian and pastor, Karen Westerfield Tucker, who experienced several miscarriages.[1] It can be adapted for use in a memorial service either at a church or in your home. Parts of it also could be used as a service within your regular church service.

GATHERING

WORDS OF GRACE *(one of more of the following:)*

> Blessed be the God who consoles us in all our affliction,
>   so that we may be able to console those who are in any affliction
>   with the consolation with which we ourselves are consoled by God.
>   (2 Corinthians 1:3a, 4)

Thus says the Lord:

> A voice is heard in Ramah, lamentation and bitter weeping.
> Rachel is weeping for her children;
> She refuses to be comforted for her children, because they are no more.
>
> (Jeremiah 31:15)

The Lord is merciful and gracious,
> slow to anger and abounding in steadfast love.

As a father shows compassion to his children,
> so the Lord shows compassion to the faithful.

For the Lord knows our frame, and remembers that we are dust.

But the steadfast love of the Lord
> is from everlasting to everlasting upon the faithful,

And the righteousness of the Lord to children's children,
> to those who keep his covenant and remember to do his
>> commandments.
>
> (Psalm 103:8, 13–14, 17–18)

PRAYER *(one or more of the following:)*

Life-giving God,
> your love surrounded each of us in our mothers' wombs,
> and from that secret place you called us forth to life.

Pour out your compassion upon *mother's Name.*

Her heart is heavy with the loss of the promise that once took form in her
> womb.

Have compassion upon *Names of father and/or other family members.*

Their hearts are also heavy with the loss of promise.

They grieve the death of the hopes *they (she)* anticipated,
> the dreams *they (she)* envisioned, the relationship *they (she)* desired.

Give *them (her)* the courage to admit *their (her)* pain and confusion,
> and couple that confession with the simplicity to rest in your care.

Allow *them (her)* to grieve, and then to accept this loss.

Warm *them (her)* with the embrace of your arms.

Knit together *their (her)* frayed emotions,
> and bind *their (her)* heart(s) with the fabric of your love for *them (her).*

In the strong name of Jesus Christ we pray. **Amen.**

Lord, we do not understand why this life,
> which we had hoped to bring into this world, is now gone from us.

We only know that where there was sweet expectation,
> now there is bitter disappointment;

where there were hope and excitement, there is a sense of failure and loss.

We have seen how fragile life is,

and nothing can replace this life, this child, whom we have loved
before seeing, before feeling it stirring in the womb,
even before it was conceived.
In our pain and confusion we look to you, Lord,
in whom no life is without meaning, however small or brief.
Let not our limited understanding confine our faith.
Draw us closer to you and closer to one another.
Lay our broken hearts open in faith to you
and in ever greater compassion to one another.
So raise us from death to life; we pray in Christ's name. **Amen.**

Ever-loving and caring God,
we come before you humbled by the mysteries of life and death.
Help us to accept what we cannot understand,
to have faith where reason fails,
to have courage in the midst of disappointment.
Comfort *mother's Name*, who has lost a part of herself,
and *Names of father and/or other family members*.
Help *them (her)* to see the hope of life beyond grief.
Through Jesus we know that you love all your children
and are with us always.
Let us feel that presence now as we seek to live in faith,
through Jesus Christ our Lord. **Amen.**

SCRIPTURE READING

WITNESS
Pastor, family, and friends may briefly voice their feelings and Christian witness. Signs of faith, hope, and love may be exchanged.

PRAYER *(one or both of the following may be used:)*

Lord God, as your Son, Jesus, took children into his arms and blessed them,
so we commit this child *Name* into your loving care.
Grant us the assurance that you have received this life, which you gave,
and grant that when we stand before you
we might be as innocent and trusting as little children. **Amen.**

Compassionate God,
soothe the hearts of *Name(s)* and enlighten *their (her)* faith.
Give hope to *their hearts* and peace to *their lives*.
Grant mercy to *all members of this family (her)*
and comfort them with the hope that one day we shall all live with you,
through Jesus Christ our Lord. **Amen.**

Here or elsewhere in the service a familiar and beloved hymn of comfort may be sung.

THE LORD'S PRAYER

BLESSING

An Annual Service Open to All Women and Families

This service is based on one that was created for Central United Methodist Church, Florence, South Carolina. The Words of Grace are the same as some of those in the "Service of Hope after Loss of Pregnancy." The responsive activity is very important. It gives all persons who are attending an opportunity to place their child's name on a permanent structure, as well as giving them a concrete remembrance to take home. Supplies for this version of the service include a memorial sculpture (garden sculptures that look like cupped hands reinforce the Isaiah passage), permanent pens (gold and silver were used at this particular service), smaller smooth stones suitable for writing a name on (one for each participant), elements for Communion. Even if your tradition does not typically use written orders of worship, it can be good to have a nicely printed bulletin for participants to take home and save.

GATHERING

PRELUDE *(Musical)*

WORDS OF GRACE

> Thus says the Lord:
> A voice is heard in Ramah, lamentation and bitter weeping.
> Rachel is weeping for her children;
> she refuses to be comforted for her children, because they are no more.
> (Jer. 31:15)
> Blessed be the God who consoles us in all our affliction,
> so that we may be able to console those who are in any affliction
> with the consolation with which we ourselves are consoled by God.
> (2 Cor. 1:3a, 4)

OPENING PRAYER

> We bring you different afflictions, O God.
> We grieve because we have lost cherished pregnancies.

Some of us grieve because we cannot become pregnant again.
Some of us grieve because of the ways our loss has changed our
    closest relationships.
Some of us grieve because of the ways our loss has affected our
    relationship with you.
We bring you different emotions, O God.
We are hurting in complicated ways.
Some of us are angry, with our bodies, with our family members, with
    you.
Some of us are confused, by our own emotions or by those of our
    loved ones.
Some of us are wondering if you even exist, and if so, if you care.
We bring you different burdens, O God,
But most of all, we bring you ourselves.
Do not leave us comfortless.
Amen.

PROCLAMATION

PSALM 130 *(Read Responsively)*

SCRIPTURE LESSON   *(this or another could be used)*   Romans 8:22–27, 31–39

SONG OF PREPARATION

SCRIPTURE LESSON   *(this or another could be used)*   Isaiah 49:13–16a

HOMILY/MESSAGE   *(an example of a homily on the above texts is included later in this chapter)*

RESPONSIVE PRAYER

Prayer Response:
    Trust in the Lord forever,
    For the Lord is the Rock eternal. (Isa. 26:4)

Gracious God, even when everything seems to be falling apart around us and within us, you are the Rock of our salvation, the most trustworthy, sturdy thing in our lives. Even when we are angry with you, even when we can't see you or feel you, even when we beat against you with tired arms and hurting hearts, you remain steadfast. We give you thanks.

    Trust in the Lord forever,
    For the Lord is the Rock eternal.

We pray for those who are hurting tonight, those who have come seeking hope and comfort from your hands.

Trust in the Lord forever,
For the Lord is the Rock eternal.

We pray for those who have suffered the pain of miscarriage, helplessly saying good-bye to conceived children they loved. You have called children in the womb by name, and we know that tiny lives, too, are precious to you. Grant these grieving parents strong comfort and assurance that the lives they lost will never be lost to you.

Trust in the Lord forever,
For the Lord is the Rock eternal.

We pray for those who feel trapped in their grief, who cannot see a way forward from the magnitude of this loss. We know that you are the source of all consolation. Inspire people to offer patient love and comfort to those who are hurting. Allow the curtain to lift, so that the grieving ones you love might sense your presence and know that they are not alone.

Trust in the Lord forever,
For the Lord is the Rock eternal.

We pray for all those in our networks of relationship who have been affected by this loss—for spouses, parents, grandparents, and close friends. Maintain and heal these relationships so they might be a testimony to your love that accompanies us through the floodwaters.

Trust in the Lord forever,
For the Lord is the Rock eternal.

We pray for the children we have loved and lost. Their lives were mysterious to us, but known fully to you. Hold those dear lives in the hollow of your pierced hand, safe and whole in your eternal presence.

Trust in the Lord forever,
For the Lord is the Rock eternal.

And now, dear God, we receive these moments as time to offer individually our prayers to you, naming those we have loved and commending them to your care, speaking aloud in this holy space the needs we have for hope and healing. . . .

Trust in the Lord forever,
For the Lord is the Rock eternal. Amen.

RESPONSE TO GOD'S WORD

HOLY COMMUNION

TIME OF PRAYER AND INSCRIBING OF NAMES
*During this time, you will be invited to come and receive Communion as
you feel led. Either before or after you receive the elements, you may kneel
at the altar for as long as you like. Please use the gold and silver pens at
the altar to inscribe a name both on the Hands of God sculpture and on one
of the stones. The name might be your name or a name you've given a lost
child. In either case, we will prayerfully commit the owners of these names to
the strong and trustworthy love of God. The sculpture will be placed in our
church's prayer and memorial garden, while the stone is yours to keep.*

SENDING FORTH

HYMN

BENEDICTION

A Service in the Home

*This service also can be adapted for use as an annual service of remem-
brance and candle lighting, to be held on the anniversary of the loss or on
the anniversary of the baby's due date. You can select either a memorial
activity or the candle-lighting litany below, or use both. Look over the service carefully ahead of time to gather any supplies you'll need: music and
speakers, for example, or the supplies you will need for your memorial act
or for the candle lighting.*

GATHERING
*(Soft music could be played as you and any other persons participating
gather and sit silently for a moment of prayer. It may be most comfortable to
sit on the floor in a circle or to circle chairs so that you can see each other
during the service.)*

OPENING PRAYER
Faithful God, we have gathered to remember the life of *Name,* and to testify
to your grace even in the midst of loss.

Our child's life was brief, but it changed us.
As we remember, help us be gathered in again with all your children, across time, across space, across every division.

Give us the comfort of knowing that you are with us, even until the end of the age. Amen.

TIME OF REMEMBRANCE

During this time, participants may take turns sharing words of witness. It would be appropriate to talk about any of the following things: your memories of the pregnancy or miscarriage; how you feel about the loss now; how you have experienced God's presence (or absence) since that time; the ways in which you may sense that God is at work through your experience of loss; your hopes for the future.

TIME OF PRAYER

During this time, participants should take turns sharing the ways in which they currently need prayer from one another. Then, one at a time, the participants should kneel or sit while the other people present place their hands on them and take turns praying aloud for them. This may feel awkward if it is an unusual practice for your family, but it can be a very powerful act of healing. You may end with the Lord's Prayer, if you choose.

MEMORIAL ACTIVITY

At this point, families can select a meaningful memorial act. Suggestions are found in chapter 13; they include writing a family letter to the lost child or to God, creating a memorial box, writing your first family letter to a child you plan to sponsor, planting a tree, or doing an activity of your choice. Let this be as formal or as informal as is natural and right for your family.

LITANY AND CANDLE LIGHTING

If you choose to include the candle lighting, take time beforehand to choose a beautiful or special candle that can be set aside for the purpose. If other children are included, you might like to let them try dipping or molding a unique candle; supplies are available at most craft stores. Make sure you have something with which to light it and a candle plate or other holder.

Leader: God has promised that nothing, not even pain or death, can separate us from God's love.

All: We belong to God.

Leader: When life brings pain, when our hearts break, God promises never to leave us.

All: We belong to God.

Leader: In a world that sometimes seems dark and hopeless, Christ is our light.

All: We belong to God.

Leader: (lighting candle) The Light shines in the darkness, and the darkness will never overcome it.

All: Thanks be to God. Amen.

CLOSING PRAYER

Compassionate God, we know you are with us, even when we have trouble feeling your presence. Care for our lost little one. Care for us in our grief. Help us care for one another with love and patience. And help us look to you—praying earnestly, loving faithfully, always searching for signs of your Light in the lives we lead. In the name of that Light, the One who gave his own life so that we might live, we pray. Amen.

A Service for Use on a Worship Pilgrimage

If you choose to take a worship pilgrimage, probably the biggest decision you will have to make is about your destination. Think of a place that is meaningful to you, preferably a place where you have experienced the presence of God. It could be the mountains or the beach, the dunes or the woods, the desert or the state park. Or it could be the church where you were married, the chapel of the university you attended, or the place you went on your honeymoon. No matter the destination, think about why you want to go there, why it is a sacred place for you. You may want to enlist someone's help planning the details of the service. This service is less detailed than some of the others. This is intentional. Use the particularities of the place toward which you are going on pilgrimage to shape your prayers and the things you do.

You will also want to decide whether you wish to go alone or have loved ones accompany you. All of us need prayer times in our "closets," and all of us need one-on-one time with God, but two things about memorial services that can bring deep healing are others' acknowledgment of the reality of the loss and the creation of shared memories.

Pilgrims have always prepared carefully for journeys. Any spiritual practices would be appropriate during the time leading up to your travel: different modes of prayer, fasting, reading Scripture, serving other people, or any of the other means of grace Christians have discovered to offer themselves to God.

GATHERING

As you approach and arrive at your destination, prepare for worship. Are you walking along a trail? Are you driving down a winding road? Have you reached the church you've chosen? Slowly and gently, allow yourself to be aware of your surroundings. Be quiet for some moments and allow yourself to seek God's presence. Pray for God to make Godself known to you.

OPENING PRAYER

You may use the following prayer or pray freely in your own words.

> Gracious God, *I/we* have come.
> *I/We* have journeyed to this place that is holy because you have met
>   *me/us* here before.
> Meet *me/us* here again.
> Touch *me/us* with your grace.
> Assure *me/us* that you have not abandoned *me/us*.
> Make *me/us* aware of your presence, aware of your love.
>   Amen.

TIME OF REMEMBRANCE

This will look different depending on whether you are alone or with others. If you have come with other people, the description of the time of remembrance for the "Service in the Home" above will be apt. If you have come alone, spend several moments reflecting on those topics, either silently or speaking aloud to yourself.

TIME OF PRAYER

Again, this will be different with company than alone. Be real about what you need from God, what you need from other people. And as you offer your raw, real self to God, allow the Holy Spirit to pray with you and to shape your prayer. You may discover that you need something you didn't realize you were lacking, or that you are angrier or sadder or more disillusioned than you thought.

Time of Listening to God

This, of course, is a continuation of prayer. But use your surroundings, the pilgrimage site you have chosen, as an icon to discover God's presence, God's word for you. Look around you. What do you see? Listen. What do you hear? What about this place holds meaning for you? Why do you think you were led to journey here? Rest in this time of listening and don't rush through it. Wait upon the Lord, and allow the Holy Spirit to whisper to you.

Memorial Activity

Any of the suggestions in the above service would be appropriate. You may have chosen to go on a pilgrimage precisely because it made possible a particular memorial act: scattering ashes, for example, or releasing a butterfly, planting a certain kind of plant, lighting a prayer candle. You could also use the litany of candle lighting included above.

Closing Prayer

> God of mercy, you are always ready to answer us when we cry out to
>   you.
> Thank you for being present with us today, and during our hour of need.
> Lead us along paths of healing.
> Give us grace so we may love without fear.
> And bring us, along with those we have loved and lost, at last into your
>   heavenly kingdom:
>   Secure in your eternal presence,
>   Freed from the days of mourning,
>   Knowing fully the extent of your love for your children,
>   You who died so we might live.
>   In Jesus' holy name we pray, Amen.

SERMONS (COMPLETE)

This sermon was written and preached by the Rev. Meghan Gage-Finn at the memorial service my peer group held for my own loss on July 25, 2003.

Second Corinthians 1:3–5; Luke 17:11–19

We have spoken the word "loss" and "lost" today, and we will hear it again before our time together closes in this service of remembrance and celebration. It is a word we are familiar with and call upon to describe what Chris and Elise have experienced and what we all experience in letting go of or losing our hold upon what we have known. We use these words when what we have been preparing for is suddenly gone, and we speak of it when we release our grip upon something we love.

We use it to mean passing away, but we can also use "loss" in circumstances to connote a sense of deficit, defeat, a shortfall.

But we cannot use the word "loss," as familiar as it may be in our vocabulary, to describe something that is in fact *found* . . . it is wrong to use "lost" to describe something, or someone, who has been claimed, who has been embraced, welcomed, nurtured, taken hold of. A thing cannot be lost if we know where it has gone, and Mabel Anne has gone to be with Jesus.

Yes, Mabel Anne has been lost to us here on earth, to Chris and Elise, but she has been found by her God who knows this baby and cares about the life of this child. She was real to Chris and Elise, a mystery becoming reality, and she still is and will always be a real . . . mystery, but nobody more than God knows how real she is, how *found* she is.

God, the Mother and Father of us all and of our Lord and Savior Jesus Christ, is, as Paul's Letter to the Corinthians reminds us, the Father of mercies and the God of all consolation. The God who knows and understands all of our afflictions and sufferings is the very same God in whom we find the community in which healing and celebration can occur. Jesus called the ten lepers who kept their distance, who were pushed out of the community and denied acceptance, and made them clean, and he says to the one who was found to return, "Get up, for your faith has made you well." And that is what we turn to in time of crisis and loss, it is where our comfort is found; we turn to our faith in one another through our faith in Jesus Christ.

God cares about each and every one of us; each of God's children is precious in the Creator's sight, just as Mabel Anne is precious and knows the love of her God.

In our "loss," God understands our anger and confusion, our sadness and fear, our feelings of guilt and brokenness. Through all afflictions, the God of mercy and consolation does not leave us lost, alone in this place of sorrow and shadows.

But through God's amazing grace, when once we were lost, we will be held as *found.* Our blindness becomes sight and we will see hope, we will see the peace that surpasses all understanding, we will see resurrection.

I cannot claim to know why, to know why Mabel Anne was *lost* here on earth.

I don't know that any of us has the answers, nor can I claim to imagine all of the questions each of us personally harbors in the waters of our hearts and prayers. What I can claim, what we can all proclaim, is our unity in the body of Christ, our communion with Christ and with one another. In our sorrow and in our perplexity we find strength in one another, committing ourselves to one another and to those we love, committing ourselves to God's unfailing care.

Mabel Anne is not lost, but is found in God's eternal care and love, just as we are found in communion with one another in God's care. We are found when we trust in God's loving mercy.

God's peace be with you.

To God be the glory. Amen.

I wrote this sermon for a community service for healing after infertility, miscarriage, or stillbirth. It was originally preached on February 19, 2009, at Central United Methodist Church, Florence, South Carolina.

"Can We Trust in Love?"

Romans 8:22–27, 31–39; Isaiah 49:13–16a

> Sing for joy, O heavens, and exult, O earth;
>   break forth, O mountains, into singing!
> For the LORD has comforted his people,
>   and will have compassion on his suffering ones.
> But Zion said, "The LORD has forsaken me,
>   my Lord has forgotten me."
> Can a woman forget her nursing child,
>   or show no compassion for the child of her womb?
> Even these she may forget,
>   yet I will not forget you.
> See, I have inscribed you on the palms of my hands.

The LORD has forsaken me, my Lord has forgotten me.

The journey through infertility can be a lonely one. You feel as if you're surrounded by pregnant people, people who say things like, "Well, I'm just a fertile Myrtle!" and "He just *looks* at me and I get pregnant!" You turn to online support communities, because after all, who else can understand the feeling of buying pregnancy tests in bulk, after TTC cycle #63? And church is less comfortable than ever before, with all the children's programs and nursery services, and well-meaning people asking, "Isn't it about time for you to start a family?" Not to mention the whole God thing, trying to pray to a God whose Bible says "children are a blessing from the Lord" in one breath and "God had closed Hannah's womb" in the next.

The Lord has forsaken me. The Lord has forgotten me.

And then there are those of us who started pregnancies, maybe easily, maybe with months or years of prayers and tears, but who found that pregnancy is no guarantee of a baby. One in four pregnancies will miscarry, ending before the twentieth week, but no one told you that ahead of time. And the precious breath of promise that started changing your body and your life, the tiny heartbeat that you sensed and maybe even saw growing inside you, died, taking with it your hopes and your joy . . . and perhaps your trust in God, the God who supposedly knits together in wombs. People who want to help batter your ears with comments like, "Oh, you're young, you can have more children," or "At least you were only eight weeks along."

The Lord has forsaken me. The Lord has forgotten me.

Some of you are here bearing another kind of loss. Maybe you suffered through a stillbirth, or had an infant so prematurely that she or he could not survive. Your hands and arms seem to bear the traces of that small body, and it's excruciating to see small children the age your baby would have been who are healthy and thriving. Maybe you had a funeral, or maybe you didn't even get to see your child. Your empty arms yearn to be filled. And people who want to help say things like, "Well, God just needed another little angel in heaven," which makes you hate this needy God who stole your child.

The Lord has forsaken me. The Lord has forgotten me.

In the midst of her own exile, Zion cries out these words of betrayal and abandonment. The Israelites have been ripped from their homes and scattered across the other nations, places that are strange and foreign, places in which they are slaves or servants, outsiders. And it's been years now. Long, lonely, heartbreaking years, with no end in sight.

But the Israelites don't cry out, "We are so tired of exile!" They don't say, "We want to go home!" or "We want our lives back!" Instead, they come right to the essential core of the whole thing. "The Lord!" they cry out. "The Lord has forsaken me! My Lord has forgotten me!" Because, really, this is what it boils down to. If you've come tonight, you're in exile of a sort. You're wandering in a place of pain, and this service is being held to help you name that pain. It's part of healing to cry out the name of what is hurting you. "I want to have a child!" "I have to know that my lost little one will be cared for!" "I want my baby back!" But all these symptoms of our exile beg the core question: "Where are you, God?" Have I been abandoned? Have I been forgotten? Am I forsaken? Because if so, if God has left the building, then hope is truly dead, and despair will be our bedfellow.

Has the Lord forsaken me? Has my Lord forgotten me?

Hear how the prophet Isaiah answers that question:

Can a mother forget her nursing child,
or show no compassion for the child of her womb?
Even these she may forget,
Yet I will not forget you.
See, I have inscribed you on the palms of my hands.

You who are here are in a position to understand this statement of God's love more than most people. Can a mother forget her nursing child and have no compassion on the child of her womb? You who are here cannot forget even the babies you *haven't* nursed, the babies you have lost. They fill your minds and your hearts and your very being. And God says, my love is even more sure, even more steadfast, even more trustworthy. I will not, cannot forget you.

Don't believe me?

Look, I have inscribed you on the palms of my hands. You. Your name, and your name, and yours. Your hearts and your hopes and your sorrows. Here, carved into my flesh, written into my very being, indelible and deep. I cannot forget you because I have made you part of me. And nothing in this world can ever get in the way of my love.

My love.
My love that sustains you through the storms.
My love that weeps at your side as you cry out in the night.
My love that holds you in your fear and comforts you in your sadness.
My love that comes to you in the listening ears and loving arms of your
    spouse, your family, your friends.
My love that is stronger than the rocks that hold back the ocean.
My love that is shown in my hands
    Pierced by nails
    Holding out bread and wine
    Written all over with the lives of my children.
    Have I forsaken you? Have I forgotten you?
    Look at my hands, and you'll see the truth.
        Nothing can separate my children from my love.

SUGGESTED SCRIPTURE LESSONS, HYMNS, AND OTHER RESOURCES FOR WORSHIP

In 1989, Share published a book of resources for planning worship and memorial services titled *Bittersweet . . . hellogoodbye*, edited by Sister Jane Marie Lamb. This book is out of print, but you may be able to find it used online or in some libraries.

Scripture Lessons

Any of the psalms in chapter 8 would also be appropriate.

Psalm 23	The good shepherd
Isaiah 25:6–9	God will wipe away every tear
John 14:1–6a	Jesus goes to prepare a place for us
Romans 8:18–27	Creation suffers; the Spirit helps us pray
Romans 8:28–39	Nothing can separate us from God's love
Romans 14:7–9	Whether we live or die, we are the Lord's
1 Thessalonians 4:13–18	We don't grieve as those who have no hope
Revelation 21:1–4	A new heaven and a new earth

Hymns and Songs

Research about the history of these hymns and songs can be surprisingly helpful, as you discover what the authors were experiencing at the time.

Traditional Hymns

"Out of the Depths I Cry to You" (Martin Luther)

"By Gracious Powers" (words: Dietrich Bonhoeffer, trans. Fred Pratt Green; music: Charles Hubert Hastings Parry)

"I Want Jesus to Walk with Me" (African American spiritual)

"What a Friend We Have in Jesus" (words: Joseph M. Scriven; music: Charles C. Converse)

"Nearer, My God, to Thee" (words: Sarah F. Adams; music: Lowell Mason)

"Be Still, My Soul" (words: Katharina von Schlegel, trans. Jane Borthwick; music: Jean Sibelius)

"O Love That Wilt Not Let Me Go" (words: George Matheson; music: Albert L. Peace)

"Jesus, Lover of My Soul" (words: Charles Wesley; music: Joseph Parry)

"Jesus Loves Me" (words: Anna B. Warner and David Rutherford McGuire; music: William B. Bradbury)

"Children of the Heavenly Father" (words: Caroline V. Sandell-Berg, trans. Ernst W. Olson; music: Swedish melody)

"Abide with Me" (words: Henry F. Lyte; music: W. H. Monk)

"Hymn of Promise" (Natalie Sleeth)

Contemporary songs

"Blessed Be Your Name" (Beth and Matt Redman)
"Held" (Natalie Grant)
"Visitor from Heaven" (Twila Paris)
"Praise You in This Storm" (Casting Crowns)
"Cry Out to Jesus" (Third Day)
"Peace Be Still" (Rush of Fools)
"You Never Let Go" (Matt Redman)
"Small Enough" (Nichole Nordeman)

Permissions

Notes

CHAPTER 1: REMEMBERING YOUR PREGNANCY

1. Table 1-6, Mean Age of Mother by Live-Birth Order, according to Race and Hispanic Origin of Mother: United States, 1968–2000, http://www.cdc.gov/nchs/data/statab/t001x06.pdf (accessed June 25, 2009).

CHAPTER 3: THE DAYS AFTER

1. Some states have laws ensuring the parents' right to the miscarried body of their child. For a partial listing of states and laws, check www.adamssong.net/state.

2. Your partner will be living through his own experience of grief, a grief that will be different from yours, which may make communication between the two of you difficult. Please see chapter 9 for a more detailed discussion of the ways in which miscarriage can affect couples.

CHAPTER 4: THE MEDICAL BASICS OF MISCARRIAGE

1. However, if you are bleeding, a good guide is to skip sex for two weeks after the bleeding stops, and check in with your doctor.

2. Bruce Young and Amy Zavatto, *Miscarriage, Medicine, and Miracles: Everything You Need to Know About Miscarriage* (New York: Bantam Dell, 2008), 272.

3. In extremely, extremely rare cases, a normal fetus may develop. Such cases require careful screening throughout the pregnancy but have been known to result in live births. Fang-Ping Chen, "Case Report: Molar Pregnancy and Living Normal Fetus Coexisting until Term; Prenatal Biochemical and Sonographic Diagnosis," *Human Reproduction* 12, no. 4 (1997): 853–56.

CHAPTER 5: WHY DID GOD LET THIS HAPPEN?

1. I wonder if there is a hint here that perhaps those who live in the space before birth have ways of relating to God that are not available to the rest of us.

CHAPTER 6: WHAT ABOUT THE BABY?

1. Serene Jones, "Rupture," in *Hope Deferred: Heart-Healing Reflections on Reproductive Loss*, ed. Nadine Pence Frantz and Mary T. Stimming (Cleveland: Pilgrim Press, 2005), 61.

2. John D. Zizioulas, *Being as Communism: Studies in Personhood and the Church* (Crestwood, NY: St. Vladimir's Seminary Press, 1985), 184.

3. Ibid.

CHAPTER 7: CONNECTED TO THE LIFE OF GOD

1. From Rory Cooney, "One Is the Body," in *Gather Comprehensive*, 2nd ed. (Chicago: GIA Publications, 2004), 612.

2. Martin Luther, "Comfort for Women Who Have Had a Miscarriage," in *Luther's Works*, vol. 43 (Philadelphia: Fortress Press, 1968), 247–50.

3. Richard Hays, in his commentary on 1 Corinthians, notes the oft-overlooked passage that reads: "Otherwise, what will those people do who receive baptism on behalf of the dead? If the dead are not raised at all, why are people baptized on their behalf?" (1 Cor. 15:29). He writes, "However unsettling we may find it, this passage serves as one more piece of evidence that Pauline soteriology is far less individualistic than Christians since the Reformation have usually supposed and that Paul is at least open to believing that the community can act meaningfully on behalf of those who are not able to act on their own behalf." Richard Hays, *First Corinthians*, Interpretation series (Louisville, KY: John Knox Press, 1997), 267.

4. L. Serene Jones, "Hope Deferred: Trinitarian Reflections on Infertility, Stillbirth and Miscarriage," *Modern Theology* 17, no. 2 (April 2001): 227–45.

CHAPTER 8: RELATING TO GOD AFTER A MISCARRIAGE

1. Justo González, "A Hispanic Creed," in *Mil voces para celebrar: Himnario Metodista* (Nashville: Abingdon Press, 1996), 70.

2. Dietrich Bonhoeffer, "By Gracious Powers," trans. Fred Pratt Green.

CHAPTER 9: WHO ELSE IS HURTING?

1. Fiona A. Murphy, "The Experience of Early Miscarriage from a Male Perspective," *Journal of Clinical Nursing* 7 (1998): 326.

2. Norman Brier, "Grief following Miscarriage: A Comprehensive Review of the Literature," *Journal of Women's Health* 17, no. 3 (2008): 451–64.

3. Daniel H. Grossoehme, "The Experience of Miscarriage: One Father's Reflections," *The Journal of Pastoral Care* 49, no. 4 (Winter 1995): 429–30.

4. Brier, "Grief following Miscarriage."

CHAPTER 11: WHEN OTHER PEOPLE SAY HURTFUL THINGS

1. C. Mansfield, S. Hopfer, and T. M. Marteau, "Termination Rates after Prenatal Diagnosis of Down Syndrome, Spina Bifida, Anencephaly, and Turner and Klinefelter Syndromes: A Systematic Literature Review," *Prenatal Diagnosis* 19, no. 9 (September 1999): 808–12. According to this research, conducted in Europe, 92 percent of parents confronting a diagnosis of Down syndrome elected to abort the child, while 58 percent of Klinefelter parents chose abortion.

CHAPTER 12: LONG-TERM EFFECTS

1. Norman Brier, "Anxiety after Miscarriage: A Review of the Empirical Literature and Implications for Clinical Practice," *Birth* 31, no 2 (June 2004): 138–42.

2. Ibid., 141.

3. Ibid.

4. Richard Neugebauer, "Depressive Symptoms at Two Months after Miscarriage: Interpreting Study Findings from an Epidemiological versus Clinical Perspective," *Depression and Anxiety* 17, no. 3 (2003): 157–60; Neugebauer et al., "Preliminary Open Trial of Interpersonal Counseling for Sybsyndromal Depression following Miscarriage," *Depression and Anxiety* 24, no. 3 (2007): 219–22

5. Kristen M. Swanson, "Predicting Depressive Symptoms after Miscarriage: A Path Analysis Based on the Lazarus Paradigm," *Journal of Women's Health and Gender-Based Medicine* 9, no. 2 (2000): 191–206.

6. Brier, "Grief following Miscarriage," 452–53.

7. Ibid., 454.

CHAPTER 13: HOW TO SAY GOOD-BYE

1. Meghan's sermon is included in the resources in chapter 14.

CHAPTER 14: RESOURCES AND GETTING HELP

1. Karen B. Westerfield Tucker, reprinted from the United Methodist *Book of Worship*. Please attribute properly any portions you use. Copyright information is on p. 161.